3-2-1- Launch© For Start-Ups

Taking your Idea from Concept to Reality

3-2-1- Launch©
For Start-Ups

Taking your Idea from Concept to Reality

By Donald E. Ball, M.B.A., CGBP®

Dedicated to
Lauran, Chris and Lacey who have
shown me love, patience, support and
forgiveness on my journey to complete
this book.
You are much loved.
Thank You.

3-2-1-Launch for Start-Ups
Taking your Idea from Concept to Reality
© 2014 by Donald E. Ball
ISBN-13:978-0990538905

Contents

Foreword

(WHY YOU SHOULD BUY ONE COPY OF THIS
BOOK FOR YOURSELF, AND ANOTHER FOR
SOMEONE YOU LOVE.)

When I was first asked to write the Forward to
this amazing book, I first had to "check my ego at the
door." Having spent nearly 50 years as an
entrepreneur, both successful and unsuccessful, I
wanted to approach this book as if I knew very little
about being an entrepreneur. And, after reading every
word, I learned that I didn't know as much as I
thought I did. But, let me go back a few years, to
when Don was working on his own agency business.
That's when another entrepreneur, Jackie Dryden,
first introduced Don to me.

From that first "hello", I knew that there
was something about Don that made me immediately
become aware that I should stay connected to him, in
some way. There was this…"fire in his belly" that no
one was going to be successful in extinguishing.

There was no way that Don was going to fail
at anything…a lot like me. Except for one
thing…both Don and I were on our way to becoming
failures at what we were attempting to do, at that
time. Yep, he failed, but rescued himself. And, so did
I.

That is a true trait of a "real entrepreneur". We
get our knees scraped and egos bruised, but we don't
stay down for long. There are too many opportunities
in "them-thar hills", and no one is going to keep
us from them.

Since that time, Don and I have nurtured a 20+
year relationship, and at times, have been brutal
honest with one-another. We have hit each other
below the belt, from time to time, and we've come
back for more. You see, every so often, you need to
have someone else keep you from drinking too much
of your own "Kool Aid". And that is what Don and I
have been to one-another.

Today, both of us have reached our vision of
success, and still we reach out…not for ourselves, but
to help others. That is what Don has achieved by
completion of this book.

The difference between this book and every other
book on becoming an entrepreneur is this: This book
will help you to talk yourself out of it, as quickly as it
will try to help you through it. Why does Don
do this? As an entrepreneur, you too will need to
perform your own self-analysis (which he clearly
demonstrates in this book)…and, yes…it's going
to hurt. You will perform a S.W.O.T. analysis upon
yourself, first. You will learn to become brutally
honest with yourself. This book will help you to
achieve an honesty you have never before known.
And, you need this.

There is an exercise that one of my mentors,
Tony Lupo, taught to me. He said: "Every morning,
look at yourself in the mirror and tell yourself what
you are going to accomplish that day. Then, before
you go to bed, in the evening, again look at yourself in
the mirror and face the truth of the day. You see,
YOU are the only person you cannot fool, nor lie
to. Why? Because YOU know the truth…and, you
cannot lie to yourself."

That was life-changing for me. I think it will do
the same for you. Now that you can no longer fool
yourself or lie to yourself, you are ready to begin to
become a successful entrepreneur.

Read every word in this book. If you miss
anything, you are fooling yourself.

Read every word in this book, because Don has
taken 40 years of his life, creating what you will soon
learn, is one of the most important books you will
ever read.

Every step you need to take, to
becoming successful…is in this book. Skip one step,
and you will trip…you will fall, and you will fail.

Don, again, you have humbled me, and honored
me. Thank you, for writing "3-2-1-Launch® for Start-
ups. It truly will help take many people "From
Concept To Reality".
 Congratulations, to you, my dear friend. I am buying

one for every entrepreneur I know…at a discount, I
hope.

---

*Randall W Montalbano is one of the most sought-after
marketing strategists I have ever known. He has helped to
direct literally thousands of companies, during
his career. Today, he still manages Montalbano Marketing,
Incorporated (www.RandallMontalbano.com) (formerly
MonMark Group, International LLC), working with start-
ups and emerging companies throughout the US. He is also
Executive Vice President / Principal of GUI GLOBAL
PRODUCTS LTD, dba Gwee Global Products,
(www.GoGwee.com) based in Houston, Texas. In addition to
this, he still has time for others, as the Marketing
Mentor/Guru for the Mid Michigan Innovation Center, a
business incubator and think-tank, in Midland, Michigan
(www.MMIC.us).*

Preface

As a small business consultant I realized that I was starting from square one each time a new client came into my office and asked how they could "start their own business". Building on a concept I developed in my first business, "The 5M's of Marketing Success©", I expanded and then proposed the same basic approach to these prospective entrepreneurs. I believed that what worked for these start-ups would probably work for others. The approach gave them structure and organization-a process for moving from concept to reality.

I found that Entrepreneurs who are serious about starting a business, as well as those who are growing their small business, are in need of a simple, straight-forward, process for converting their idea from a concept to reality. They seemed to agree.

This book presents a concise method for *"Taking Your Idea from Concept to Reality"* ©. It is based on the stages of the 3-2-1- Launch© Process which are:
- Situation Analysis
- Feasibility Research
- Plan
- Fund
- Launch
- Stabilize
- Grow

- Exit

To reap the greatest good from this book, it should be read through to understand the overall process, then re-read again and applied to your business idea.

Good luck. Let me know how it goes...

Don Ball

Acknowledgements

While this book presents my suggestions and recommendations for those starting a business, the views presented are based on the concepts and observations I have had over the last 40-plus years. And those observations are the result of many friends, and especially family, who have helped me to learn and grow through the years. Although there are many whose paths I have crossed who have impacted my personal, spiritual and professional life, I especially want to express a sincere "Thank You" to:

My Family- Lauran, my wife of over four decades, who has supported my efforts in the entrepreneurial world even though she would be the first to say, "Get a job and keep a job!" And, thanks to my children, Chris and Lacey, and their families, who have been there for me when things got tough-and in the good times, too.

My Business Partner, Marvin Howard, who jumped, blind-folded into the deep end of the entrepreneurial pool thinking that one day we'd both be rich small business owners. Little did we know that there is more than one way to define rich!

Thanks, also to those who have helped and encouraged in other ways: Charmaine Valencia who helped edit the early versions; Dr. Jimmy Adams who kept pushing me to finish the book; The UH-SBDC and the Lone Star College System-SBDC who gave me the opportunity to fine-tune the processes that I developed during my first attempt at the small business ownership-especially Sal Mira who encouraged me to keep learning and searching for the answers and was there when I needed guidance in helping my own clients; and to the Lone Star SBDC Team who have shared their insights into the entrepreneurial world.

I'd also like to thank those from my church congregation who have supported my education and my family during the rough times that entrepreneurship presses upon us. Running a business is not something that one does on their own-but with the help and support of so many others.

I'd especially like to thank all my clients who have trusted me to help them move forward with the accomplishment of their dreams to become a small business owner. I truly appreciate your confidence and I pray great successes in your future. Thanks for all you taught me as we both took this journey together.

Thanks, mostly, to God who guided me to this point in my life. He blessed me by surrounding me with just the right family (physical and spiritual) and the right friends and clients to enable me to provide guidance to others.

In the beginning...

In May, 1982 I was laid off as manager of an in-house ad agency at an oilfield service company. For weeks management had asked me to trim my department budget and when it got down to three salaries (mine, my Creative Directors' and the Administrative Assistant's) I decided it was time for a talk with the boss. I explained that while I was not advocating a lay-off, if one was pending I'd appreciate an opportunity to present a proposal to become a consultant and handle their advertising on an outsource basis.

He suggested that I put the proposal together!

So, with the help of my Creative Director, Marvin Howard, I proposed that we become their ad agency at a rate considerably below market value (Frankly, I didn't even know what market value WAS then and I had no idea what to charge for our time- but I made it worth the deal.)

On a Friday morning two weeks later we both were part of a "reduction in force" (translated "you're out of a job...!"). Friday afternoon the proposal was accepted and signed and on Monday morning Marvin (now my partner) and I came back to the same offices as President and Vice President of our own advertising agency. The company even agreed to let us use office equipment and the receptionist would answer the phone for us.

"Wow", I thought, "starting a business is easy". It wasn't until years later that I realized that _"Starting"_ a business and _"Building"_ a (successful) business were two different things-and one of the toughest jobs one could ever undertake.

The business lasted three years. The first year we were profitable (how many start-ups can say that?). The second year the business "broke even". The third year the business was approaching bankruptcy. I hired my first attorney that year-frankly, to get me **_out_** of business. I also met some very interesting people from a government organization called the IRS.

By this time the relationship with my family was strained. We had young children and I spent little time with them. After all, I was "self-employed" and "President of my own company!" I had full responsibility for the company's success. If it was successful, my family would be taken care of. If not...well, we wouldn't think of that. Fortunately, I had a wonderful wife and children that cared about our family enough to see us _all_ through it.

We've been married forty-plus years now, and I attribute the longevity of our marriage to having a great, loving, honest and (especially) forgiving wife. She told me it was time to get out, but I wouldn't listen. The harder I tried to make things right, the worse things got.

On top of that, the then popular show *"Thirty-Something"*[1] presented the plight of two young guys who were trying to start and run a successful ad agency. Marvin and I watched the show faithfully every week. You can imagine the mood in the office the day after the leads in the story announced they were closing down the agency. "How could they?" we exclaimed. "This is OUR future you are talking about". Ironically, the two stars of the show merged their ad agency into another agency (which we eventually did, too) and the principal was forced to fire his former partner…a real twist because I was forced to "lay-off" Marvin years later in another agency. Talk about truth being stranger than fiction!

What was simply a television show for "dramatic entertainment" had become very real for the two of us.

Fortunately, with the help of a team of specialists (CPA and Attorney), we were able to shut down the business without filing for bankruptcy.

So what happened?

---

[1] "Thirty-Something" (an American television drama about a group of baby boomers in their thirties that was created by Marshall Herskovitz and Edward Zwick for MGM/UA Television Group (through United Artists Television) and The Bedford Falls Company, and aired on ABC.)

We understood advertising. We understood trade shows (we focused on the trade show market). We understood the creative approach. But, *we didn't know anything about running a business.*

What did we learn?

- There is more to being in business than simply doing what you like to do. I was bitten by the "entrepreneurial bug". I determined that if it was difficult for me to be successful, I'm sure that it was difficult for others. Now I understand why the failure rate for small businesses is so high! I wondered if there were a good, simple, straight-forward process for taking an idea from concept to reality. I wasn't afraid of hard work and long hours. I had already incorporated both into my work ethic (just ask my family!).

- Our clients taught us that they not only wanted our marketing services; they also wanted to be guided through the process carefully and systematically. As a result, we developed the *"5-M's of Marketing Success"©*.

Subsequent jobs and business opportunities over the next 25 years (I've had more than 20 "jobs" in my 40 year working career) never doused the flames of desire to be a successful entrepreneur. I was even more "independent" at each job I took. I looked outside the box for different ways to do things and was labeled "the guy who relied on forgiveness rather than permission". I marveled at those who were successful as entrepreneurs. I evaluated my "Strengths" and "Weaknesses" and looked at the "Opportunities" (and I sure saw a lot of those!) and the "Threats" that stood in the way of being a successful entrepreneur. (I never really could see the threats clearly. But then, entrepreneurs rarely do.)

What was my focus? Why had God allowed me the opportunity to experience what it was like to be "Self Employed"? I finally realized God had used those 20-odd jobs to train me to help others be successful. I became a Senior Consultant with the SBA's Small Business Development Center. That opportunity resulted in my expanding the 5-M's of Marketing Success© into a process that could help others start and launch their small businesses successfully.

I asked, "What if I could develop a method for *defining an idea* and doing the right *research*, then develop a *plan* (based on the research) and then obtain the funding to *launch* the business?"

But it couldn't stop there. Once the business had been launched, it needed to have processes and then to *stabilize* those processes and the organization. There are always things we learn after we've started a project that we wished we'd known ahead of time-it is true that experience is a valuable teacher. So, setting up the right check-points to monitor and address the primary aspects of the business to insure it will grow is critical to its long-term success. Then, what about *growth?* And, eventually, *exit.*

For some, starting and running a successful small business is second nature. But for others, starting a small business represents a maze of strange activities, stresses and financial aspects they had no idea even existed. Making the transition from an employee to the business owner is tough!

Working with hundreds of clients further solidified my original *"5-M's of Marketing Success"©* into the *"3-2-1-Launch ©Process."* It was designed to be:

- A simple, straight-forward, process to help an entrepreneur and business owner understand the steps to business success;

- A way to keep the business owner focused on the task at hand and to avoid distractions and false starts; and,

- A method to increase the confidence of the entrepreneur and business owner by assuring them that there is a method and process for achieving the success they want.

But there was one more component that I learned was necessary for success. I believe Christian Entrepreneurs have an added source of power and guidance for the success of their businesses. It's called the Spiritual Dimension.

The Business of Small Business

The impact on the economic health of the country by small businesses is well documented. According to the U.S. Small Business Administration Office of Advocacy, September 2010 FAQ[2], there are an estimated 27.5 million small businesses (a small business is typically defined by the SBA as having fewer than 500 employees and no more than $7 million in average annual receipts) in the United States. These businesses:

- Represent 99.7 percent of all employer firms
- Employ half of the country's private sector workforce
- Hire 40 percent of high tech workers, such as scientists, engineers and computer workers
- Pay 44 percent of total U.S. private payroll
- Generated 65 percent of net new jobs over the past 17 years
- Include 52 percent home-based businesses and two percent franchises
- Represent 97.3 percent of all exporters of goods
- Produce 13 times more patents per employee than large patenting firms.

In addition:

- Self-employment tends to grow as the economy falters, which is especially true among laid-off workers who start tiny companies after failing to

---

[2] U.S. Small Business Administration Office of Advocacy, September 2010 FAQ

find work in slow times. (*Source: USA Today, July 17, 2005*)

- Where do small business owners go for advice? 52 percent from individual mentors; 51 percent from social networks; 44 percent from trade associations; 36 percent from business advisors; 31 percent from the Internet and 27 percent from Chambers of Commerce (*Source: American Express*)

What is the role of women, minority, and veteran entrepreneurs?[3]

- Of the 27.1 million nonfarm businesses in 2007, women owned 7.8 million businesses, which generated $1.2 trillion in revenues, employed 7.6 million workers, and paid $218 billion in payroll. Another 4.6 million firms were 50 percent women owned.

- Minorities owned 5.8 million firms, which generated $1 trillion in revenues and employed 5.9 million people. Hispanic Americans owned 8.3 percent of all U.S. businesses; African Americans, 7.1 percent; Asian Americans, 5.7 percent; American Indians and Alaska Natives, 0.9 percent; and Native Hawaiian or other Pacific Islanders, 0.1 percent.

- Veterans owned 2.4 million businesses in 2007,

[3] Source: U.S. Dept. of Commerce, Census Bureau, Survey of Business Owners; Advocacy-funded research by Open Blue Solutions, 2007 (www.sba.gov/advo/research/rs291tot.pdf), and Office of Advocacy: The Small Business Economy (www.sba.gov/advo/research/sbe.html).

generating $1.2 trillion in receipts; another 1.2 million firms were 50 percent veteran owned. About 7 percent of veteran business owners had service-connected disabilities in 2002.

- In 2008, the overall rate of self-employment (unincorporated and incorporated) was 9.8 percent, and the rate was 7.1 percent for women, 7.2 percent for Hispanic Americans, 4.7 percent for African Americans, 9.7 percent for Asian Americans and Native Americans, and 13.6 percent for veterans. Service-disabled veterans had lower self-employment rates than non-service-disabled veterans.

Seniors in Business[4]

Entrepreneurship among seniors is growing. In 2002, the rate of self-employment for the workforce was 10.2 percent (13.8 million workers), but the rate for workers aged 50 was 16.4 percent (5.6 million workers). Although those age 50 and older made up 25 percent of the workforce, they comprised 40% of the self-employed. Solo business formation in the future will be driven by people who take early retirement or whose jobs just disappear.

---

[4] AARP/Rand Corp. "Self-employment and the 50 Population"

What is the survival rate for new firms? [5]

- Seven out of 10 new employer firms survive at least 2 years, half at least 5 years, a third at least 10 years, and a quarter stay in business 15 years or more.

- Census data report that 69 percent of new employer establishments born to new firms in 2000 survived at least 2 years, and 51 percent survived 5 or more years. Survival rates were similar across states and major industries.

- Bureau of Labor Statistics data on establishment age show that 49 percent of establishments survive 5 years or more; 34 percent survive 10 years or more; and 26 percent survive 15 years or more.

So, small business is really BIG Business. And, Americans should applaud and support those who take the risks of starting their own businesses.

For additional information, go to www.SBA.Gov/advo and www.SCORE.org.

---

[5] U.S. Dept. of Commerce, Census Bureau, Business Dynamics Statistics; U.S. Dept. of Labor, Bureau of Labor Statistics, BED.

Overview of the 3-2-1-Launch Process

What is it?

- A simple, straight-forward, process to helping an entrepreneur and business owner understand the steps to business success;

- A way to keep the business owner focused on the task at hand and to avoid distractions and false starts;

- A method to increase the confidence of the Entrepreneur/ Business Owner by assuring them that there is a process for achieving the success they want.

Simply stated, entrepreneurs need all the help they can get! They are entering a new phase of their lives and they need guidance, mentoring and a focus on details that they may never have experienced.

That's why the 3-2-1- Launch© Process was developed… To serve as a guide through each step of the entrepreneurial process so the new business owner can focus on what is important at each stage of development and so they will be prepared for the challenges and opportunities of the future. Successful entrepreneurs are not just risk takers; they are "Educated Risk Takers".

The stages of the 3-2-1- Launch© Process are:

- Situation Analysis
- Feasibility Research
- Plan
- Fund
- Launch
- Stabilize
- Grow
- Exit

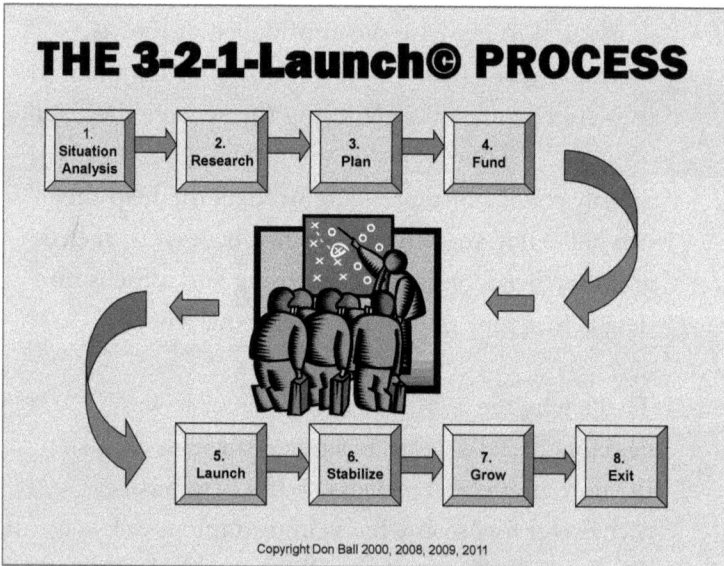

THE 3-2-1-Launch© PROCESS

1. Situation Analysis
2. Research
3. Plan
4. Fund
5. Launch
6. Stabilize
7. Grow
8. Exit

Copyright Don Ball 2000, 2008, 2009, 2011

Stage 1: Situation Analysis

THE 3-2-1-Launch© PROCESS

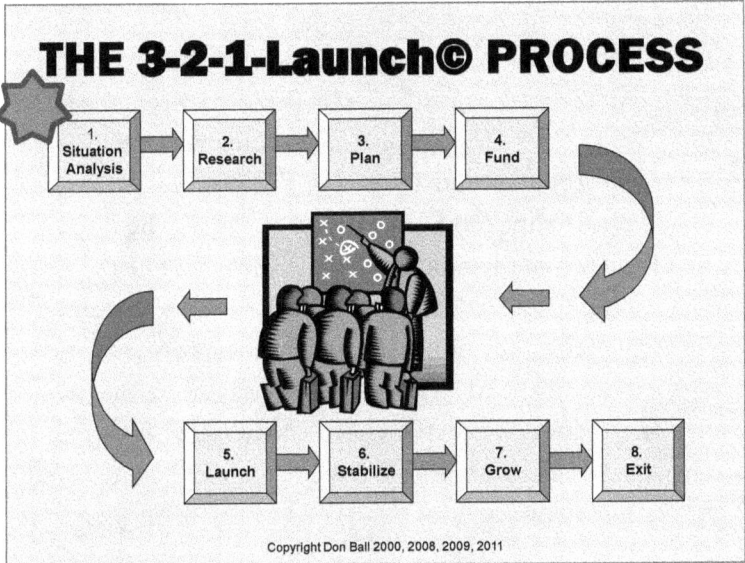

Copyright Don Ball 2000, 2008, 2009, 2011

The first stage of starting a business really centers more around you than the business. Successful entrepreneurs are not just risk takers; they are "Educated Risk Takers". They consider all aspects of a business idea and how it will impact their lives and then make the decision of whether or not to start a business. While the decision may not always be right, it should be based on a combination of personal considerations and business information.

The Objective of this Stage is to determine if you are the kind of person that can be successful as an entrepreneur and to evaluate how the business opportunity you are considering will affect you and those around you. Basically, you will analyze your situation, identify some options and develop a "Concept".

There are two parts to this stage. The first requires that you look inward-at your Personal Strengths and Weaknesses. The second helps you analyze the Opportunities and Threats of the Business Opportunity. And, the reverse could also be true-analyze your personal opportunities (You just received your cosmetology certificate) and threats (there are a lot of people getting their cosmetology certificates) and analyze the business strengths (no hair salons with experienced cosmetologists in the area) and weaknesses (I have no experience managing a hair salon.)

Personal Strengths and Weaknesses

The idea is to determine how your personal strengths and weaknesses will impact your ability to start and operate a business? Why is it important to take a close look at yourself, first, before starting a business?

Consider the survival rate for new firms:

"Seven out of 10 new employer firms survive at least 2 years, half at least 5 years, a third at least 10 years, and a quarter stay in business 15 years or more."[6]

---

[6] Source: U.S. Dept. of Commerce, Census Bureau, Business Dynamics Statistics; U.S. Dept. of Labor, Bureau of labor Statistics, BED.

Motivation

Let's start by looking at your motivation for starting a business. Let me begin with a story about a client who came to me with an idea to establish a Yoga and Wellness studio. It quickly became apparent that she had an intense desire to establish a venture that would help others in their quest for physical and emotional well-being. Her motivation did not center on the financial rewards of the business (In fact she didn't even achieve profitability in the first two years!) but she had a desire to really help others.

What is motivating you to consider starting a business? Where is your passion? Do you have a hobby? Do you think you can make a business from your hobby?

The reasons that people start businesses are numerous, but those reasons can usually be categorized into two groups: "PUSH Motives" and "PULL Motives."

A *PUSH* Motive is something that is *pushing* you to start a business, usually by some outside event, like losing a job and not being able to find another. A *PULL* Motive is *enticing* you to start a business, usually driven by an opportunity or personal influence, like having an idea or a new product.
In short, PULL Motives are typically driven by your passion (As in the example of my client above). Of course, a PUSH Motive can become a PULL Motive when you start investigating and researching the

possibilities of starting a business and become excited about the prospects.

PUSH Motives include:

- Lost job: Perhaps you have lost your job and cannot find another one. Today's economic situation has forced millions into the ranks of the unemployed. Many people cannot find a job and are turning to entrepreneurship as an alternative option. But is that reason enough to start a business?

- Someone else's Idea: Sometimes entrepreneurs become business owners at the encouragement of someone else. "If we work together, maybe we can do this. You have one skill and I have another…" When starting a business venture, especially with someone else (and especially if it is a family member), carefully evaluate not only your own motives, but the motives of your "partner."

PULL Motives include:

- Idea: Maybe you have an idea for a service that others need, or a product you have been working on and are now ready to "take to the market." I have had clients tell me "I have this idea that I cannot stop thinking about, and I believe I could make some money if I did it the right way…"

- Filling a Need: Perhaps one of the greatest business start-up drivers is seeing a need and having a determination to find and offer a solution I worked with a client who wanted to start a daycare for children and adults with disabilities-because her own son had some mental issues and it had been a challenge to find quality care services for him.

- Desire to "Be your own Boss": If I had a nickel for every time I've heard "I've always wanted to be my own boss" and "Starting my own business will give me a chance to see if I can do it"... I would be rich. Do you really know what it means to be your own boss? Ask someone who is. Your hairdresser, the corner convenience store operator, or the guy who does your lawn work. Ask them to tell you three good things about being the boss, and three things they've learned since they have become "the boss" that they wish they had known before they started the business. The responses will probably surprise you.

- Time: Perhaps you have time. Maybe you are recently retired and want to do something productive with your time. Maybe you want or need an additional source of income. Just remember that business ownership takes much more time than most entrepreneurs anticipated. Just ask any business owner! I recently asked a client with an existing business how he was doing and he responded: *"I'm doing ok. I feel like I'm at a super critical point in my company's development, it feels like I'm in a wrestling match."*

- Customers: Another major PULL Motive is when you actually have customers who are ready to buy a product or service. Having customers is great, but the key is knowing how many customers it will take to be successful and how you will find them.

33

- Family: Some entrepreneurs just want to take charge of their future and realize that they will never be happy working for someone else. They want to provide a higher standard of living than their family is accustomed to, or perhaps they want to take charge of their finances in a way that will insure their children have money for college.

- Money: The thought of making a lot of money (or at least enough money to pay the bills) is really appealing to some. But, you need to be realistic.

Consider your level of personal development per Mazlow's hierarchy of needs.

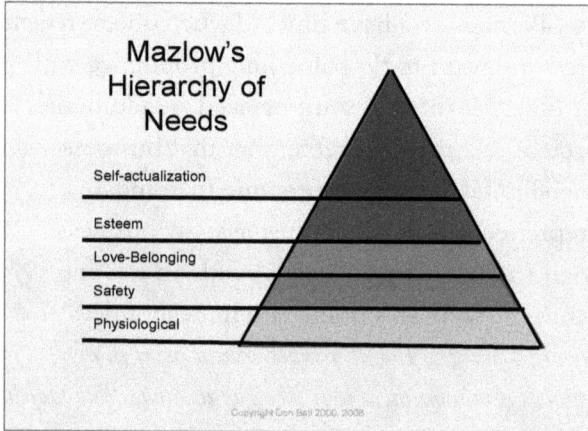

Your motive for starting a business is what will get you up in the morning (and keep you up at night!), so you should think about it very seriously. If your motive is a PUSH Motive, you may want to rethink whether business ownership is right for you because you are starting the business based on the action someone else made (i.e. losing your job and not being able to find another one).

A note about the correlation between "starting your own business" and "making a lot of money": There is no question that there is a lot of appeal in the idea of making a lot of money and being your own boss. However, just because you are your own boss does not necessarily mean you will make a lot of money. Two sisters who wanted to open their own hair salon drafted a business plan which indicated they would not take home a cent until the second year,-and then it was less than minimum wage. Their motivation was to be their own boss and to service the needs of clients who were encouraging them to start the company.

So, consider your motives for starting a business very seriously. Why is having a motive so important? Because you will need to rely on those motives to get you through the rough spots…and there WILL be rough spots!

Some additional items to consider include:
- What did you want to be when you grew up?
- How does that goal compare to what you would like to do with the rest of your life?
- What are your key values?
- When your life is ending, what will you regret not doing, seeing or achieving? What will you be most proud of?

Employment

Becoming the owner of your own business is like applying for a "job." You need to evaluate your strengths and weaknesses in terms of your work skills. Do a self-evaluation of what you like and do not like about your job (or the jobs you have had). What brought you satisfaction? Do you have good people skills? How about organizational skills? Are you good with numbers? What did you enjoy doing on the job and what did you NOT enjoy doing? What would you do differently if you were the boss, and why? If you have such good ideas, why doesn't the boss implement them?

Maybe you have always dreamed about forming your own accounting business. This is fine if you have strong accounting skills. But, if you have poor people skills, it might be difficult for you to find new clients for your business. It is important to understand your strengths AND weaknesses. Again, be honest with yourself. Understanding the weaknesses will enable you to know where you may need some specialized training to support the areas where you are not strong. Or, perhaps you can hire someone who possesses those skills or attributes.

I had a client who asked me to help him decide what type of business he should start. We began by discussing his motivation. He had lost his job, could not find another one and decided to start a business before his money ran out, a typical PUSH motive. I asked about his employment experience and he said he had worked in construction and remodeling. After discussing other places he could go to find a job, we discussed the types of businesses he would like to start. They ranged from "something in the healthcare business," to "running a convenience store with gas pumps" to "starting a goat farm to provide meat to local area meat markets." I encouraged him to do some additional research on the options before he invested any money in a new business venture. He revealed in our last conversation that he had decided to buy a fried chicken franchise. Actually, this client probably should have consulted a life coach more than a business coach.

Work Experience: What is your work experience? Develop a resume listing major accomplishments. Record all the facts about your work experiences. Record where/when you have worked and your job function (not necessarily the title, but what you were responsible for doing). Indicate who you worked for and their expectations and observations of your work performance. Did the people you worked for ever indicate that you had specific strengths...or weaknesses?

- List any special requirements or skills you might have had on the job. Did you travel (where to and for how long); did you have to make presentations before groups of people, like your fellow-workers or the public; did you have a supervisory or management role; did you have fiscal responsibility for the company, a location or a department? This information will be used later when you are preparing your business plan.

- Are you currently working? If so, do you anticipate a lay-off, merger, acquisition or retirement?

- Contacts: Develop a list of major contacts that should be advised once you have launched this business. Remember to add contacts from social media sites such as Linked-In, Facebook, Twitter, etc. Do you have contacts in the work area? These will be very valuable when you launch your new venture. Organize the list and capture them on a spreadsheet or some other electronic medium like ACT™, Outlook™, or Prophet™. Having access to them electronically will be helpful as you prepare to launch your new venture. You might also want to categorize the contacts. Are they fellow workers, bankers, suppliers, etc.?

- Likes and Dislikes: What type of work have you found satisfying in the past? Record your personal observations of your work situation. Do a self-evaluation of what you liked and disliked about your jobs. What brought you satisfaction? Do you have good people skills? How about organizational skills? Are you good with numbers? What did you enjoy doing on the job and what did you NOT enjoy doing? What would you do differently if you were the boss, and why?

Look at all this employment information as if you were about to hire this person (you) to help you with your new venture. On a positive note, what would they (you) be bringing to the company (the strengths)? However, you should also consider the negatives they (you) would bring to the company (the weaknesses).

Identifying, and recording your weaknesses, is not a bad thing. Understanding the weaknesses will enable you to know where you may need some specialized training to bolster the areas where you are not strong. After all, one person cannot "do it all."

Some additional ideas to consider include:
- Record all the facts about your work experiences. (A resume is helpful)
- List your job functions.
- What words describe your employers' <u>expectations</u> of your employment performance?
- What words describe your employers' <u>observations'</u> f your employment performance?
- List any special requirements or skills you had on the job.
- Did you travel?
- Did you make presentations?
- Did you have supervisory or management responsibilities?
- Did you have fiscal responsibility?
- List words that you would use to define your work experience.

Educational Experience

Your educational background may be important in some businesses. Obviously, if you are planning to open a doctor's office or a CPA firm, your customers expect you to have attained a certain educational and professional level. The client I mentioned earlier who is planning to start a daycare for children and adults with disabilities will face clients who expect her to have a level of formal education and training in order to feel comfortable about placing their loved one in her care. Her goal is to finish her medical studies before launching her new business.

Similar to a resume, record all your educational information including when and where you went to school. List any degrees, certifications and special training you may have. Indicate the areas of study at which you were most proficient and those with which you struggled. What additional training do you feel would help you personally and professionally when you start the new venture? The client starting the daycare for children and adults with disabilities is also planning to take business classes while she gets her healthcare degrees and certifications.

Some additional items to consider include:

- Education level: What is your education level? Attach a sheet which lists your education background.
- Degrees: What degrees/certificates have you earned and from what organizations?

- Special training/skills: Do you have any specialized training or skills? List and describe.
- List any certificates or special training.
- List extracurricular activities in college.
- Indicate the areas of study where you were strongest.
- Indicate the areas of study where you were weakest.

Financial Situation

Do you have money in the bank? The current economic situation has wiped out or reduced many savings and 401k programs. What is your position to weather an extended period without income? Entrepreneurs typically face long periods with limited or no income. Can you weather these dry spells? In addition, you should consider items like health insurance, college costs, retirement planning, etc. Most lenders want to know if you can live for 6-12 months without drawing any income from the company.

Do you have the funds to finance the venture? Most lenders and investors want to see how much you will invest - usually anywhere from 10-30% before they will commit. And, they typically want to see a 700+ credit score. Ask yourself if you have enough money to start the business *and* to support your lifestyle until the business can support you.

Personal Finances: How would you describe your personal financial situation? I would suggest consulting with a Certified Financial Planner (CFP) or Advisor to gain a more comprehensive picture of your financial situation. Work with them to prepare an overview of your financial situation, such as your savings, insurance, retirement accounts, etc. Note this information as it may be necessary when you apply for a loan or perhaps for an investment. A financial planner will help you understand the need for financial planning now, as you launch and grow your business and later as you prepare to exit the business. A CFP will play a valuable role in keeping an eye on the "finish line" for you. (We'll discuss the role of the financial planner more in "Chapter Two: Feasibility Research")

Some of the specific items to discuss with your CFP include: Have you ever prepared a personal budget, stuck to it and made modifications to insure your bank account will always stay current and "in the black?" This is a good example of what it is like to establish and manage the finances of a business - only on a much grander scale. If you cannot manage your own personal budget what makes you, or a lender, think you will be able to manage the finances for a company?

Some additional ideas to consider include:
- Do you have a savings account?
- Do you have a job? If so, what is the annual compensation?
- Does your spouse have a job? If so, what is the annual compensation?
- What are your average monthly expenses?
- What is your average monthly income?

- Do you have enough money saved up to live for a minimum of 6 months before taking a salary from the company?
- What is your credit score?
- Do you have a financial planner?
- Do you have a will?
- Describe your insurance situation.
- Describe your retirement situation.

Physical Situation

Contrary to popular belief, entrepreneurs have less, not more, time to themselves after starting a business. The demands on your physical and emotional health can be stressful at best. You will be entering a new phase of your life and all the responsibility of providing a paycheck for yourself and your employees will be on your shoulders. This can be a heavy burden to carry and it will challenge you physically.

You might recall the response I received from one of my clients when I asked him "How's business?" His response was, *"I'm doing ok. I feel like I'm at a super critical point in my company's development, it feels like I'm in a wrestling match. "*

- Health issues: Do you have any health issues and if so, what are they? What kind of health are you in? Do you have diseases or ailments which require medical attention on a regular basis? How is your blood pressure and your heart rate? Do you exercise regularly? When was the last time you went to the doctor for a check-up?

- How do you anticipate your health influencing and impacting your business decisions? If you are sick frequently, you should consider whether you will be able to manage your company appropriately. The company, specifically your employees and other stakeholders such as investors/lenders, suppliers and especially customers, will expect you to be available. When you become "the boss," you simply shift the one you "report to" from your current supervisor to many others who have certain expectations of you. If you do not meet their expectations, especially those of your customers, you will not have a business for long (but you will still have the loan to pay off at the bank!)

  Bottom line, the Boss is simply the one of whom others have the greatest expectations. You will need to be in good health - physically and emotionally, to fulfill those expectations.

- Insurance: One of the big concerns for entrepreneurs is health insurance. Do you have/need health insurance (for yourself and for any others)? How do you expect to cover this expense while your business is growing? The federal government has approved legislation regarding healthcare coverage for employees. The business owner should become familiar with the legislation and consult advisors as the new program is initiated.

44

If you have health insurance utilize it BEFORE YOU GO INTO BUSINESS to get a clear picture of where you are physically, and what steps you need to take to improve your health. Starting a business with a heart condition may not be the wisest decision.

In addition, consider disability insurance. What happens if you are injured or ill and unable to fulfill the requirements of your role as the "boss?" You may need to hire someone to fill in for you, or you may need insurance to cover your own salary while you are recovering. And, do not say, "It will never happen to me…," because it can and does.

Another important consideration, when the time comes, is "Key Man" insurance. This insurance will cover losses in the event that your partner is unable to perform as expected-for whatever reason.

Some additional ideas to consider include:
- How would you describe your health?
- Do you exercise? If so, how often?
- What is your cholesterol number?
- What is your typical blood pressure number?
- What is your weight/height?
- What is your BMI (Body Mass Indicator) number?
- Do you have diabetes or some other illness?
- When was your last physical?
- Is there a history of any diseases in your family?
- Do you have health insurance?

Stakeholders

Who are the *others* who will be involved, influenced or impacted by your decision to launch a business and what are their expectations? I call these the "stakeholders." Consider the employees whom you will be hiring (and their families), the suppliers you will be using, the bank or the investors that will be providing funds to help launch your venture, those people/companies to whom you already owe money, the community where your business will be operating, and especially, your customers. Most importantly, be sure to add your own family to this list!

What is reasonable for them to expect from you and your venture? Can you deliver on those expectations? If you cannot, what will you do to meet those expectations (assuming they are legitimate and worthwhile)?

I was once counseled by a wise, experienced business owner who told me that one of the five critical components of a successful business is to have the support of your family. The other four, in no particular order are to have a CPA an Attorney, a Banker, and a "Good Idea." You will not realize the importance of having the support of your family until you face the question of whether to pay yourself or your employees, or find yourself working 20 hour days and miss your daughter's recital. Or, you have a client who does not pay on time and you cannot take home a paycheck. Or, a customer who wants you to deliver in one week instead of one month...

Don't think it will ever happen to you? I hope not, but plan for it and call me after three years and let me know how you did.

- Identification: Make a list of the people (by name) who depend on you. This includes relatives, creditors, your Mortgage Company, etc. The list represents those who would be impacted by your decision to become an entrepreneur.

- Relationship: Identify your relationship to them (i.e. Mother, sister-in-law, creditor, Mortgage Company, etc.)

- Expectations: Next to their names and relationship, list their expectations of you (unreasonable though they may be!). Spouses expect a degree of financial and physical security. What about health insurance for the kids in the event of a broken arm? A child expects you as a parent to provide a safe, healthy environment, while the mortgage company expects you to pay your mortgage on time.

  Even more significant is the time that you will spend away from your family. Do not underestimate how much time it will take to develop, launch and get a business to the "break-even point" much less to the success point...

  Some additional ideas to consider include:
- List the people for whom you have some responsibility (spouse, children, parent, etc.)

- Describe the relationship you have with your spouse in five words.
- Describe the relationship you have with each of your children in five words.
- Describe the relationship you have with your parents in five words.
- Describe the relationship you have with your in-laws in five words.
- Describe the relationship you have with your creditors in five words.
- How would those to whom you owe money describe you?
- How would your neighbors describe you?
- How would those with whom you worship describe you?
- How would your banker describe you?

Business Management Experience

Do you have specific business experience you can use to address a need in the marketplace? For instance, if you are planning to start a daycare you should have actual experience operating - or at least working in - an establishment which serves the needs of children. But, what if your experience is in keeping the books? Great, that may position you to set-up a bookkeeping business. However, if you set-up the daycare and your strength is in bookkeeping, you will find you lack much of the practical operational skills needed to be successful and you will find yourself gravitating toward the financial part of the business rather than running the business and taking care of children. If you are planning to open a welding shop, it would help if you have experience as a welder. Or, if you are opening a restaurant, having actual restaurant management (ownership is even preferred!) experience is important. I had a client who wanted to open a restaurant. She had limited skills as a restaurant manager, but had never actually OWNED a restaurant. The banks had a hard time justifying a quarter million dollar start-up loan!

- Management Strengths: What management and/or ownership experience do you bring to this venture?
- Management Weaknesses: In what areas are you weak and may be in need of some additional training or assistance?

I usually suggest to my clients that they rank their management experience in eight categories: Sales, Human Resources, Information Technology, Customer Service, Marketing, Finance, Legal, and Operations/Production. In addition to these basic business functions, a business owner should rate high in the area of: leadership, vision, organizational skills, and negotiations.

Business Opportunities/Threats:

The second part of the Situation Analysis is to evaluate the business situation. This will require that you look at the external picture. It is important to clearly define the Opportunities and Threats you will face if you decide to launch this venture.

Consider the Opportunities for your Business:

What are the Opportunities you see in the marketplace? Study the markets, industries and the competition. Obtain research on demographics, lifestyles, and habits (we'll look more specifically at Feasibility Research in Stage 2). Identify the problems and needs of the people in your community. Watch trends in clothing, communications, and changes in lifestyle patterns.

For instance, is there an opportunity to start a restaurant in an area that is growing, but has no restaurants? You can also look at "Opportunities" as "Needs." What needs exist that your business venture can address?

MSN™ recently published an article on creative business start-up ideas. Some of the ideas included: Pool man, Grass painter, Caretaker, Board-up Guys, Locksmith, The "Cleaners", and "Garage Doors Gone Wild". These were all businesses which were started in response to opportunities and needs which these entrepreneurs identified in their local areas.

Perhaps there is a need for a daycare facility to service a new subdivision or community? Or there may be a need for a service station/convenience store to provide services in an area where there are no other service stations, but there is a high traffic count? If you can see a need, and have access to the skills required to service that need, you may have a good start toward launching a successful business venture.

But beware! Just because no daycare or restaurant exists does not mean an opportunity exists for you to build one there. Maybe there is a good reason!

I had a client who wanted to move their daycare closer to the area and the parents they served. They developed a business plan, were approved for a $750,000 loan from the bank but stopped the project when they could not get approval from the local fire marshal for the design of the building even though they met the code. There was a reason why no daycare existed there - they could not get the permits and approvals!

Some additional items to consider include:
- The size of your pocketbook (Capital)
- The potential payoff
- Your knowledge and skills
- Past work experience
- Hobbies

Consider the Threats for your Business:

Like the Opportunities, Threats are external issues. What threats does your venture face, even with a strong need or opportunity? Threats could be that there are many other daycares already in business in your area. There might be some pending government legislation which could adversely affect your business. Take the study of "threats" very seriously. If you can identify the threats, you will go a long way toward identifying a way to address or mitigate the threat altogether. DO NOT IGNORE THE THREATS - THEY FACTOR INTO MAKING "EDUCATED RISKS!"

Situation Analysis Summary

Summarize the data you have gathered from the Personal Strengths and Weaknesses and the Business Opportunities and Threats by establishing:

Goals: Set the goals for the business. Ask yourself what you want this business to accomplish for you (and your family). Are you establishing this business so you will have more time for your family? If so, look seriously at your options and see if that will be the case. If you are starting the business to "make more money," be honest in your evaluation of the financial situation. Consider your motivation carefully. Can you actually make more money? Some possible goals might include:

- Goal 1 Example: Make more money
- Goal 2 Example: Have more control of my time

Metrics for Success: What metrics will you use to deem your business "successful" in 1-, 3-, or 5-years? Perhaps the metrics are financial (make more money to put my children through college), philanthropic (make money so I can participate in helping others), or health related (my current job is very stressful and I need to have a position that will result in less stress). Other traits of business owners who want to increase their chances for success:

- Trait 1: A desire to succeed which drives you to push the limits of your technical and analytical skills...
- Trait 2: A commitment to not only do things right, but to do all the right things...
- Trait 3: A desire to continue learning…
- Trait 4: Sacrifice, a willingness to give up many activities and luxuries...
- Trait 5: Motivation to be a good planner...
- Trait 6: Vision-Vision-Vision…

Barriers to Success: What will prevent you from being successful in this venture? Here are some examples:
- Barrier 1: Money- Are there financial concerns (review the evaluation you completed earlier about your financial situation).
- Barrier 2: Government regulations- Perhaps there are some government requirements that you must meet before you can launch the business.
- Barrier 3: Family support- If you do not have the support of your family it will be very difficult for you and your business to be successful

- Barrier 4: Time- A new business venture will take much more time to reach "success" than you may anticipate. Be sure you have the time to give your business a chance to succeed.

- Barrier 5: Education- Perhaps there are educational requirements such as a degree, testing or certification required before you can open for business. These must all be considered, especially in terms of the resources necessary (expense and time). Obviously, this brings up the consideration of what additional training might be necessary before you start a business. Training might include classes at the local community college on accounting, marketing, human resource management and of course, any classes on entrepreneurship.

- Barrier 6: Health- As stated earlier, your health is an important factor in the success of your business. If done right, starting a business will be much more strenuous than you may anticipate.

Options

Now list and describe the options you are *considering* based on the information you have complied thus far. Look at two aspects: The "must haves" and the "nice to have."

The "must haves" are what you determine to be essential in the options you select. For instance, based on your personal budget you determine that whatever option you select "must generate a minimum of $XXX in take home pay to cover your expenses and commitments." You may also include other items like "must have Sundays off, or "must provide the ability to pick up the children every afternoon after school."

The "nice to have" list may include similar type items, but you can be more flexible on whether, or to what degree, they influence your decision to consider an option. For instance, you may state that it would be nice to be off on weekends, but you are willing to wait until the third or fourth quarter before you actually start taking off on the weekends. You might also state that it would be nice to have a full-time bookkeeper, but you are willing to outsource the service until the company can afford a full-time employee.

So, what are your options? Start by listing the criteria for the options in the area of "Must Haves" and "Nice to have." Then list all the possibilities. For instance, you can start a business from scratch. You can buy a business which already exists and continue to operate it "under new management." Or you can buy a franchise. You can even consider a staged approach by selecting a short-term option that will lead to your ultimate objective.

Obviously, you probably do not know right now WHICH option is the best. This will require some research (which we'll go over in the next chapter). There are many options, so list the possibilities on the worksheet. Here are some examples:

- Option 1: Keep my current job
- Option 2: Launch a new business from "scratch"

- Option 3: Buy a business
- Option 4: Buy a franchise
- Option 5: Go to work for a company (i.e. "Get a job")

Summarize your situation by describing your *"Concept."*

Describe your "Concept" for this venture in terms of:

- What you will do
- For whom you will do it
- Why you think customers will pay you for the product or service, and how much they will pay
- How much money you have to invest in the venture
- How long you can live off your personal savings before taking funds from the company

Donny Deutsch has written a good book called, *"The Big Idea: How to Make Your Entrepreneurial Dreams Come True, From the Aha Moment to Your First Million"* (available in hardcover from Amazon). Write down your answers to the above considerations and then summarize them with a "Concept" statement. Ideally, you should build on your Strengths, address your Weaknesses, take advantage of Opportunities, and, plan for dealing with the Threats. Your "Concept" statement might go like this:

- (What do you plan to do?) I plan to start a Daycare Business.
- (What Strengths will this venture build on?) I am great with kids and it will give me the opportunity to

56

be with my own young children rather than sending them to another daycare while I work outside the home.

- (What Weaknesses will you address with this venture?) I recognize that this will require dipping into my savings/401k, but I believe the trade-off of being with my children will be worth it.
- (What Opportunities will you be responding to?) There are many children in the area, but no local daycare service.
- (How will you address the Threats to your business success?) I will insure that the daycare is geographically positioned to reach the greatest number of prospective customers.

Your "Concept" might be stated as:

"I plan to start a daycare on Smith Street, to address the needs of the new subdivisions being built in the northwestern section of town."

The Bottom Line...

The objective of Stage I: Situation Analysis is to evaluate your personal strengths and weaknesses in terms of motive, employment background, education, financial position, physical condition, stakeholder expectations, and business management experience. You should also consider the business opportunities and threats; develop a situation analysis that summarizes your goals, identifies the metrics for success and the barriers to success and, especially, defines the options available to you. The end result of Stage I: Situation Analysis is to select your "Concept."

Stage 2: Feasibility Research

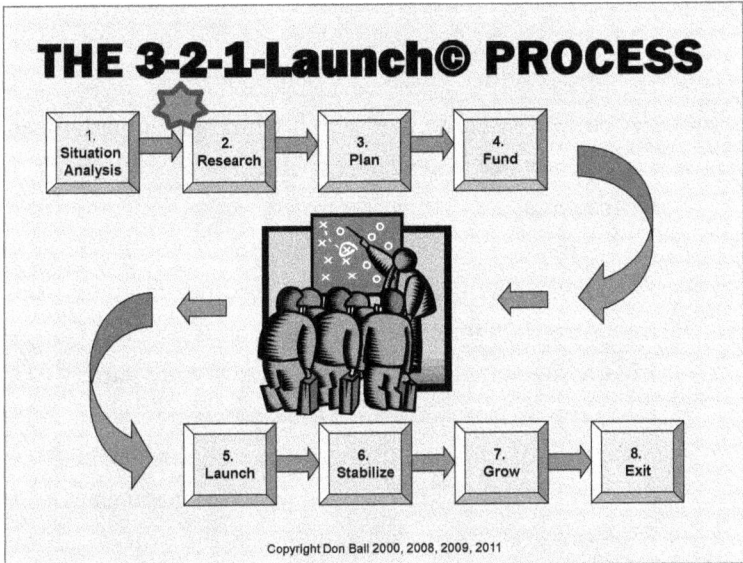

THE 3-2-1-Launch© PROCESS

1. Situation Analysis	2. Research	3. Plan	4. Fund

5. Launch	6. Stabilize	7. Grow	8. Exit

Copyright Don Ball 2000, 2008, 2009, 2011

Once a "Concept" has been selected and defined, the next step is to determine the feasibility of the idea. Is your idea able to support an entire business? If not, you may just be dealing with a hobby.

Starting a business without researching the feasibility of the idea is like building a house without knowing what is in the ground beneath it. Is it clay, rock or sand? Knowing the facts BEFORE you start building will help you build with the right design and minimize problems later.

Research

A word about research, there are two basic types of research: Primary and Secondary.

- Primary Research is original research done for a specific product, service or company.
- Secondary research is research which has already been conducted and is available in libraries, Chambers of Commerce, and other resources.

An example of Primary Research comes from one of my entrepreneurship classes. The class was for prospective entrepreneurs who had a wide variety of ideas for their businesses. One lady wanted to start a business based on a number of her cookie recipes. She declared that her cookies were "as good as Mrs. F's Cookies," a popular franchise at the time. I explained that the only way we as a class would know whether her cookies were better would be for her to let us taste them!

The next class she brought her cookies and a tray of Mrs. F's Cookies. The class was unaware of which tray was hers' and which were Mrs. F's Cookies. Everyone in the class tasted cookies from both trays and completed a short survey asking their preferences, why they preferred one over the other, and capturing demographic data like gender, age, ethnicity, etc.

The results showed that indeed her cookies WERE better, at least to those who were surveyed. Granted, it was not a scientific survey, but provided some basic data to the client which she felt would be helpful. For instance more of the men preferred her cookies, and of the women who enjoyed Mrs. F's Cookies, they preferred a particular type (chocolate chip).

This seemed like a pretty good method for explaining the difference between primary and secondary research, so I asked each new class which followed if anyone was introducing a new food product. We hit the jackpot when one gentleman revealed he had a steak sauce better than "X-1 Variety." (We tested the class and he beat-out X-1 Steak Sauce by a score of 26-25!)

Research Components

There are 10 different areas to consider when determining the feasibility of your idea. When you have completed the Feasibility Research you should be able to answer the following questions:

1. What is the need? (Motivation)
2. Who has the need and how many there are? (Market)
3. How will your company meet the need? (Magic)
4. What is the best model for your business in order to meet the need? (Model)
5. What are the requirements that must be met to meet the need? (Mandatory's)
6. What are the tools that are available to communicate your solution to those in need? (Media)
7. Who are the people necessary to establish and run the company so that it can effectively meet the needs of your customers? (Management)

8. What are the strategies you will use to meet the need? (Method)
9. What funding will be necessary to start/sustain the business and is there sufficient revenue to build a profitable business? (Money)
10. What is the schedule for developing and launching your business? (Measurement/Milestones)

Motivation

What NEED in the marketplace will your venture address? It is important to establish the Motivation behind your business. Is the motivation customer-driven (there is a need my company will address) or is it company-driven (I have a product and I want to find someone who needs it.) Companies can be started from both angles, but if there is no need, whether real or perceived, your company will find it difficult to sustain any kind of existence, much less growth.

Ask yourself what your customer's motivation is to use your products/services? Why SHOULD they buy your product or service rather than some other product already on the market? What are they using now? Surprisingly, the answer to this question is readily available. ASK THEM!

Start by determining whether the need is "REAL" or PERCEIVED." Perhaps there is a need for a daycare center, but none exists in the area. If you build one (assuming there are families in the area who are searching for a local daycare) you are responding to a need. If, however, you have a building and say, "I've always wanted a daycare center" that may be a problem - especially if there are no families with small children in the area!

The need may be "PERCEIVED". You may have heard the story about "Pet Rocks?" Gary Dahl, a savvy Advertising Executive and his friends were discussing how much they'd like to have a pet, but that there was so much "maintenance" involved (feeding, grooming, veterinary expenses, etc.). He developed a product, called a "Pet Rock" which came with the "Pet Rock Training Manual" in response to the "perceived need" in the marketplace.

Essentially, he selected rocks, polished them, glued the rocks together and glued on "eyes" and packaged them in a box, which looked like a "travelling pet container, and sold them for around $4.00. He launched the "idea" at a gift show in August and sent out thousands of news releases. *Newsweek* did a half-page story and by the end of October he was shipping 10,000 pet rocks per day. By Christmas it is reported that he had sold over a million Pet Rocks for $3.95 netting a minimum of $1.00 each.

Although the life cycle of the venture was short, it was very profitable!

Many new ventures fail to find out what their customers and prospects really want. Do they want black or blue; or maybe large or small. Their needs may be focused around delivery options or payment terms. Issues that, frankly, may have less to do with the product or service you offer than the way they receive the product or service. You will not know what they want until you ask them. You must constantly remember who is writing the check (giving you the credit card, issuing the Purchase Order, etc.).

One client I worked with was launching an Emergency Notification Service. It required a data center where information would be captured, then transmitted to a number of communication devices including land line telephones, mobile devices, email, and even fax machines. While all the buyers in the market segments (Residential, Commercial and Government) had the same interest (to be notified of an emergency as quickly as possible), the _reason_ they wanted this notification varied. Commercial buyers did not want to face the media and explain why they opted to not buy the product when it could save lives, while the residential market was looking at the fact that it could help them protect and defend their family and home in the event of an emergency. Of course, many of the residents felt the government should be responsible for notifying them and that the government should provide the devices...and thus one of the market segments (the residents) actually became an influencer on another market segment (the Government)! It is critical to know exactly what the market wants, and why.

I consulted with one client, a supplier of asphalt parking lots, who was unsure of why she was losing market share. The business had been around for over 30 years but had been losing market share to newer, start-up businesses. When I asked why customers were buying from the "new guys" rather than her business, she said it was probably because of their pricing and the fact that they had newer trucks. I then asked why HER customers bought from her, and specifically those loyal customers who had been using her company for a number of years. She responded with, "I'm really not sure, but it is probably because we've been around awhile or our prices or our guys wear uniforms..."

Her response about her own customers' motivation for buying was, frankly, no more precise than her knowledge of why other customers were buying from her competitors. She really did not know why her customers bought from her.

We decided to conduct a survey (this is a good example of "Primary Research" because we did it all ourselves) of her ten best customers. We simply asked three questions:

1. Why did you buy from us in the first place?
2. Why did you buy the second time? (They had an opinion of the company from the first project, so if they were unhappy they would have probably looked elsewhere), and,

3. What would you tell someone else about the company?

    The survey results were very surprising. Of the ten companies surveyed, nine came back with a word that the owner had never used: "RESPONSE." When I asked the owner about this she said, "Oh, that's probably because when a customer calls we have someone at their office within fifteen minutes. It's just the way we do business."

    I was surprised that she could even DO that, but it brought home a point she had never considered: Her customers saw the real value of working with her, not in the price, nor the uniforms her crews wore, but in the fact that _her company was responsive to their needs!_

    At the next trade show we focused on the "Response" angle and used a tag line of "Asphalt problems? Ask **A.R.T.**-The **A**sphalt **R**esponse **T**eam." We gave away clocks and watches to emphasize the timeliness of their service. The response (no pun intended) to her message was 300 new client prospects from a 2-day trade show!

    Another critical aspect of MOTIVATION is to determine why customers buy from your competition. How do you find out...?

    Again, ask your customers - then listen carefully to what they tell you. It may be surprising how much you can learn from your customers - especially prospective customers. Your customers may even tell you all the reasons they bought from your competitors and how pleased they are that your products/services are now available.

The Bottom Line: Talk with your prospective Customers. They are a valuable part of your marketing team!

Market

In this part of your research you will:
- Identify potential MARKET SEGMENTS
- Describe/profile the BUYERS you will be selling to
- Describe/profile the INFLUENCERS who can impact the buyers' decision to acquire your product/service
- Describe/profile the PARTNERS you can work with to reach the Buyers and Influencers
- Identify the ASSOCIATIONS/CHAMBERS and ORGANIZATIONS which can assist in reaching your buyers
- Describe/profile the COMPETITORS your venture will face (Consider size, age, product offering, etc.)

Research the MARKET. By market we are referring to prospective customers. Look at "market" as all those who need to know about your products and services and can either make, or influence, the decision to ultimately purchase.

Begin with a thorough understanding of the Industry. Is it growing, stable or declining? You can get this information by identifying and researching the appropriate NAICS code (North American Industry Classification System: http://www.census.gov/eos/www/naics) for your business. Their website describes the NAICS Code as "the standard used by Federal statistical agencies in classifying business establishments for the purpose of collecting, analyzing, and publishing statistical data related to the U.S. business economy."

For instance if you are considering starting a Beauty Salon the NAICS code and description is:

"NAICS Code No. 812112 Beauty Salons: This U.S. industry comprises establishments (except those known as barber shops or men's hair stylist shops) primarily engaged in one or more of the following: (1) cutting, trimming, shampooing, coloring, waving, or styling hair; (2) providing facials; and (3) applying makeup (except permanent makeup)."

You can then go to your local library and obtain more detailed research about that specific industry, especially in your geographic area. Ask the local librarian or SBDC Consultant to obtain a "Reference USA Report" list of other businesses in your area which have the same NAICS Code. Why? These companies are your competitors! (We'll discuss competitors in more detail later.)

Now, divide the industry into six primary components: Market Segments, Buyers, Influencers, Strategic Partners, Organizations and Competitors.

- Market Segments are different groups that could buy your products or services. For instance, the emergency notification device company referred to earlier identified three primary market segments where its device could be used (Commercial, Government and Residential).

  In the case of the Beauty Salon, the market segments would primarily be women. However, your business might focus on "Young women," or "seniors."

  Each group would represent a separate market segment. Each market segment is then divided into buyers, influencers, strategic partners and competitors. It is important in the early stages to identify what those market segments are, then rank them as most-to least-likely to buy your products and services.

- Buyers: It is critical to know everything you can about the Buyers. The Buyers in the Commercial Market Segment (Building/Property managers) were very different from the buyers in the Residential Market Segment (Homeowners). More importantly, the motivation for each to buy was vastly different as well. Similarly, the "Young Women" buyers are very different from the "Senior Women" buyers. Remember that Buyers are those who ultimately make the buying decision.

- Influencers: are those who can influence someone else to buy. Suppliers fall into this category because they know your business and products and can refer you to others who may be interested in your products and services.

- Strategic Partners: are those who insure your product or service is accessible and presented appropriately to buyers and influencers. This group is often referred to as the supply chain or distribution network.

- Organizations: Organizations are those places where you will find possible buyers, influencers, partners, and even competitors. Businesses who service a specific industry tend to form groups. Research the groups to learn more about the industry. There are trade associations for just about every subject you can imagine. If you were going to form a business selling saddles you could reach breeders and others interested in Appaloosa horses by going to: http://www.appaloosa.com/association/association.htm to learn more about the Appaloosa Horse Club. To reach a broader group, consider membership in your local Chamber of Commerce.

- Competitors are those who offer an alternative to your product or service - even though their product or service may not be the same as yours', or for that matter even similar. If the buyer perceives that it is an alternative - for whatever reason - they _are_ a competitor. For instance, the pet rocks were not really a competitor to a real pet. However, when it came to someone actually spending money on a "pet," they became a competitor because they represented an alternative. We'll address more on competition in the next section.

Now, let's put these Market components together in an example.

Assume your company manufactures and sells candy bars. Let's say Mom is in the grocery store check-out line. Little Johnny sees a candy bar he just has to have and "encourages" (i.e. throws a tantrum!) Mom to make the purchase. Obviously, Mom is the buyer because she makes the actual purchase. Little Johnny is the influencer and the grocery store is the strategic partner because it was their job to have the product in front of either the buyer or the influencer - and to know which would have the greatest influence on the sale. Note also that a supplier may have recommended that the Grocer include your candy bar in his product mix because other stores were selling a lot of your candy bars. Obviously, other companies know and understand this scenario, so Mom is faced with some buying options - thanks to your competition. And, competition includes more than just other candy manufacturers. It will also include gum and chips - alternatives to your product.

Another example is a photographer who specializes in wedding photography. Although the Buyer could be the "father of the bride" (the one who writes the checks), the Influencer (the bride) certainly has a lot to do with the decision. However, finding the bride may be difficult for a new wedding photographer. It could be advantageous for him to partner with a bridal salon that sells dresses or a flower shop that specializes in bridal floral arrangements.

Buyers (Customers) are, obviously, the most important components of any successful business. Without them you have no business. If you form a relationship with them - and maintain constant and open communications - you will be able to identify their changing needs and desires and adapt your product offerings accordingly.

You can also pick up other referral business as well when your Buyer becomes an Influencer on another buyer who hopefully influences someone else to buy, and so forth. I'm sure you get the picture and you can see why having a "satisfied customer" is so important to the growth of your business. By the same reasoning, word from a "dissatisfied customer" spreads even faster!

Without this relationship you may be surprised when your customers begin buying from your competitors! Consider adding your customers to your advisory team. (We'll talk more about the advisory team later.)

Other factors that impact the Target Market include an understanding of the demographics (The characteristics of human populations and population segments, especially when used to identify consumer markets - Source: The American Heritage® Dictionary of the English Language,), psychographics

(The use of demographics to study and measure attitudes, values, lifestyles, and opinions, as for marketing purposes - Source: <u>The American Heritage® Dictionary of the English Language</u>.)

The Bottom Line: Clearly profile the market segments in terms of buyers, influencers, strategic partners and competitors and know the quantity of each!

Magic

Now that you know something about the industry, the buyers, and their motivation and needs, it is important to understand how the buyers currently address their needs. What products do they currently use and where do they obtain them? In this step, conduct thorough research on your competitors to determine what and how you can compete with them. The idea is to develop a profile of what the buyer wants that the competitor is ___**not**___ providing.

That means developing a product to address the target buyer niche.

- Describe each product (definition, price, features, benefits, production time, COGs %, etc.) you plan to offer.
- Identify the legal protection required for the product (Trademark, Copyright, Patent) and at what cost?
- Will you require a prototype and, if so, how do you plan to produce it and at what cost?

Looking back at the emergency notification device company the list of competitors was extensive. Some competitors serviced all three market segments while others only serviced one or two of the segments. It was critical to know who the competitors were, what they offered, and why their customers preferred their product/service over other products.

The company developed a profile on each competitor and included information on: products, pricing, placement (where and how the buyer could obtain the product), promotion (where and how they promoted the products) and people (who they used to sell their product - a sales force, via the internet, etc.). This is typically referred to as the distribution system/network.

The information was critical in the development of a product that the buyer would purchase.

Price isn't always the reason a client buys one product over another. Some residential customers used a "weather alert unit" which could be purchased for under $20 but was often unreliable. In areas where tornados and storms were a real threat, a reliable product was not just a preference, but a necessity. Therefore, promoting the reliability feature was more important than having a lower price. In fact the market was willing to pay considerably more for a product that "guaranteed reliability."

Consider packaging, also. Some clients may want to buy your products individually, while others may want them bundled and delivered. Take a restaurant for example.

A couple opened a small Bar-B-Que (BBQ) restaurant with great tasting food. They planned to focus on walk-in traffic, but soon were being asked, because of the quality and friendliness of their service, whether the BBQ was available on a catering basis. They researched the catering option, by providing inquiry cards on the tables, by the cash register and in the bags for take-out. They eventually expanded their services to include catering services-based on the responses from their customers.

It is important to ask your prospective customers what THEY consider the true Features, Advantages and Benefits (FAB's) of the products and services available from your competition. You might be surprised at how little they may agree with your competitor's claims! Using the example of the emergency notification device, let's look at the differences.

Features describe the tangible, physical aspects of your product (e.g. Small compact box; Large screen, etc.) while *Benefits*, as defined by the online "Business Dictionary," are "Actual factor (cost effectiveness, design, performance, etc.) or perceived factor (image, popularity, reputation, etc.) that satisfies what a customer needs or wants. *Advantages* present a position of superiority, comparing your product against other, competitive products with statements like costs savings, and delivery options.

Although it is critical to know the Features and Advantages of your product or service, frankly, customers do not buy Features and Advantages. They buy BENEFITS. They ask, "How will the purchase of this product or service benefit me, my company, my family?" If you, as a seller, cannot answer that question, your clients may not be able to answer it either, resulting in no sale, or a purchase of your competitors' product/service.

Another aspect of Magic (products and services) is to clearly identify the costs, schedules and suppliers involved with producing the products. New businesses should manufacture prototype units and test them with prospective customers before going into mass production.

I worked with a company which had developed a product for dispensing chemicals into sprayer tanks in the agricultural industry. We manufactured a number of prototypes and took them for demos to prospective customers. The very first customer praised the product but asked why we were trying to sell the product to a specific market when there was a much larger market that would eagerly buy the product if it was only modified slightly. The modification was slight, and relatively inexpensive, yet positioned the company for greater, quicker success.

The Bottom Line: Do not develop a product then go looking for someone to buy it. Develop and market products and services that your customers want to buy. Get them on your design team.

Model

Research the business model options that are available to you. We have already addressed this in Stage I-Situation Analysis, but it is worth revisiting here. What Model will your venture follow? Consider:

- Start your own business - This will require that you do all the work. There is no model for you to follow - or if there is one, it requires a degree of editing and modification. If your business is successful, it will be to your credit. If not, guess who gets the blame? Not surprisingly, it may be easier to get funding for a venture with a proven business model, like a franchise.

- Start a home-based business - Home based businesses are becoming very popular, based largely on their low cost of entry. There are some tax advantages too, since you may be able to "write-off" a portion of your home for business expense. Be sure to get an accountant or CPA to help you understand the legal and tax implications.

- Buy an existing business - There are businesses for sale that may be a very good option for you. Consider using a business broker who knows how to evaluate a business and negotiate the right kind of deal for you. Do not go it on your own here!

- Buy a franchise - Franchises are very popular because they represent a business idea with a proven track record of success that can be verified before you buy into the program. It is recommended that you consider using a Franchise Broker to assist you in finding the right kind of franchise. Note that the government has set very stringent requirements on the franchisor regarding the disclosure of information about the franchise. Hire a broker to help you get through the paperwork. It will be well worth the expense!

Write down a description of the model you want to follow, i.e. "A "start from scratch" restaurant combining the convenience of "Subway®" with the "whole foods approach of "HEB®" grocery store."

You should also research and determine the most appropriate legal structure for the business (LLC, Sub-S Corporation, etc.) and the associated costs. Meet with your CPA or Attorney for assistance in this area.

The Bottom Line: Select the right model for your business that will enable you to address the needs of your customers most effectively for them and most profitably for you.

Mandatories

List any requirements the company/staff/product must meet or have to operate. For instance, are there any special permits, certificates or licenses you must obtain before you can start the business? How long will it take to obtain them and at what cost? The best way to anticipate this is to look at the requirements for each department-prior to opening the business.

Mandatories are not just limited to the legal department. For instance, the engineering department must meet certain requirements to function within Local, State and perhaps Federal guidelines. The Finance Department may be responsible for obtaining a sales tax permit. Marketing is responsible for developing a Logo/Brand and a website before you open the business. Make a list of mandatories by department, including the "Management Department."

The Bottom Line: Know the requirements for your company to produce and provide its products and services-before you launch the business.

Media

What marketing media tools are available to communicate the Message to the Market about the Magic? A lot of entrepreneurs get caught up in how they will promote their business.

They might say, "We'll definitely have business cards and a website," or, "Maybe we should have a billboard or a booth at the industry trade show, and we'll take a serious look at social media."

While these are all viable methods for communicating information about a company's products and services, it is important to consider a few things before you select the way you communicate the message to the market.

Consider the following:

- Identify the Media tools available to promote the products/services and the company. For example: website, trade show booth, yellow page ad, brochure, uniforms, social media, etc., and those which are most appropriate to promote your venture.

- What are the rates for each media tool?

- How will you establish your brand?

- It is important to establish, and then remain consistent about how the brand and your message are displayed. Do not change colors and designs. Choose one design and stay with it.

- Apply your design to as many of the senses as possible.
    - Sight - Logo, colors, type fonts, images, structure

    - Smell – such as you experience when you enter a coffee shop

- Touch - There is one popular bathroom tissue supplier which focuses on the softness of their product by showing those who are buying the product squeezing the package. It forms an impression in the mind of the buyer (and the influencer, too!).

- Sound - One local Houston home foundation repair business has used radio for years to promote its company's message. They always follow the name with a "bumping" sound. (Sorry I cannot illustrate it better, but that's the point!)

Use every one of the senses you can to establish your brand.

- Financial aspects: Consider the cost to design, produce and present your message using each of the different media. Some will enable you to get your message out faster (i.e. Twitter and Facebook), while others, such as your website, may take a while longer to produce and update, but can have a more lasting impression. The frequency with which the message should be delivered can have an impact on your media budget as well. Presenting your message just once is not sufficient, unless you are buying an ad on Super Bowl Sunday…and few start-ups can afford the price tag for that form of advertising!

- Competitor media programs: How does your competition promote its products and services?

The Bottom Line: Learn as much as possible about the marketing Media tools that are available so when you prepare your marketing plan you can use the most effective tools for your specific product and services to reach your target market.

Management

This step requires that you consider the "people" aspects of your business. As you consider how you will lead your company, there are two groups you will call on for advice.

- Mentors: I recommend you identify some individuals who have your best interests at heart and ask them to serve on your Advisory Board. They want you to succeed and will be honest and forthright with you when you face tough business decisions. Select individuals you respect for their integrity and business and industry experience. You might think about adding one or more customers who like your business idea and want to be a part of helping you launch a successful venture.

Think back to Stage I - Situation Analysis where you identified your personal strengths and weaknesses. Surround yourself with experienced, competent advisors and mentors who can bolster your weaknesses and enhance your strengths. But remember that members of your Advisory Board are NOT your employees. Respect their time and resources.

- Key Managers: The second group consists of the professionals you will hire, either as employees or as contractors. Prepare an organization chart and identify the professionals you will hire to manage each department -whether internal or on an outsource basis (Sales, Marketing, Finance, Legal, HR, IT, Customer Service and Operations/Production). They are professionals within a given area (marketing or finance, perhaps).

When I meet with a new client, I draw a circle and then divide it into eight sections. Other than it obviously looking somewhat like a target (which is appropriate!), I explain that the circle represents their company. They, as the owner, are in the middle. I, as their advisor, coach and counselor am right there in the middle with them. However, even with my suggestions and recommendations and what I think is very credible, valuable advice, the circle still belongs to them. It is their company and they are ultimately responsible for whatever happens.

Then I explain that the eight sections represent the eight key managers they need to have on their "Core Team". These eight core team members coincide with the eight departments in a business: Sales, Marketing, Finance, Legal, Human Resources, Information Technology, Customer Service and Operations.

While there are certainly others who can be added like insurance and real estate specialists, these are the core group. Although some entrepreneurs may possess some of the skills (accounting, or marketing perhaps), I have never found a client with all these skills. Having these people on your core team right from the research stage can be a valuable asset as you develop and launch your business.

One more area to consider: Your competition. Look at your competition. How are they organized? What do you know about the ownership, the management team, and how they recruit and train their staff? Research your competitors to get as detailed a profile as possible about each company.

Taking what you have learned about the competition, ask how you will structure your own company. Can you draw an organization chart? Lay your chart over each of your competitors' organization charts and note the similarities and differences. It is not necessary to duplicate what your competitors are doing, but it is good to learn from them. If they have an operations manager and you do not, ask why? Are you planning to handle the same function in a different way? Perhaps you can accomplish the same tasks with fewer people. That will certainly help with the cash flow situation in your business.

Now, how will your company be organized and for what tasks will each department be responsible? Develop a preliminary organization chart for how the company will be structured initially and how it will evolve over time.

Take a look at each of the departments in your proposed company and (re)define the mission for each department. Be sure to compare this list against each of your competitors. Granted, at first you will be wearing all the hats. But this exercise will help you develop a vision of what your company will ultimately look like.

It is critical to realize that the departments within a company do not function independently. Marketing must understand how IT works. Accounting must work with sales and sales must work with operations. In fact your job as the owner is to communicate company direction and insure that everyone is working together toward the same goal. You will be the "Master Communicator" and glue that holds the organization together. That is what leadership is all about - having a vision and communicating it in a way in which everyone on your team buys into it and moves forward in the same direction together. If you need to get some training in areas where you are weak, do so now, before you start the business. Even though you will have someone else managing that function, YOU MANAGE THE MANAGERS!

Welcome to business ownership!

The Bottom Line: Identify a team of mentor/professionals who have your best interests at heart. Call them. Talk to them. Ask them questions and pay attention to their advice. Surround yourself with a management team that can help you plan for, launch, and sustain a successful business.

Method

Look at the overall research you have conducted so far and develop a strategy for how you will launch and sustain your business. For example, before I could open a coaching business built around a book which describes a system for starting a business, I had to develop the system and write the book. Sounds simple, but taking things step by step is the only way to manage a task. A manufacturer may need to design and produce a prototype before they can sell any samples and certainly before a lender will provide funding for a business. You may need to identify and contract with companies you want to "rep" for, or find and negotiate a lease for your new company.

Go back to the list of "mandatory's" to be reminded of the action steps you must take before you are funded and launch your business.

Each action item should be followed by who has responsibility to complete the item, the due date and the costs that would be incurred for that item. Here are some specific strategies you should consider:

- Marketing strategy: should include Competitive, Promotional, Distribution and Pricing strategies
- Personnel strategy: Define who you will hire to fill what positions and when
- Production/Operations strategy: Explain how you will produce your products and deliver them to your customers;

- Financing strategy: Explain how you will finance your venture - loans, lines of credit, investments, or a combination
- Customer strategy: Explain how you will develop partnerships and relationships with your customers
- Management strategy: Identify the functions which each department will be required to develop such as Strategic Plan, Budget, IT, Personnel, Processes, Training, Deliverables and Reports

The Bottom Line: Develop a process and strategy for each primary component of your business and understand how it compares to that of your competitors.

Money

This is one of the most critical components of your research. This section is divided into four parts: *Revenue Streams*, *Expenses*, *Funding* and *Planning*.

- Revenue Streams take into consideration all the ways the venture can make money. This is separate from investments, loans, grants and lines of credit. List all the ways the company can make money, primarily from sales of its products and services. The company may start with one primary revenue stream and expand or add others in the future. For instance, the BBQ restaurant mentioned earlier started by making money from sales of BBQ plates inside the restaurant, but expanded to an additional revenue stream in the catering and delivery area. Eventually, the company may write and publish a BBQ Recipe book or buy a BBQ trailer and compete in BBQ Cook-Offs. Each option expands the methods of generating revenue.

- Expenses are another critical aspect of the Money equation for your business. There are two steps to identifying expenses for a business: Start-up costs (the costs you will incur BEFORE you open the doors) and Operating Costs (The costs you will incur on a regular, monthly basis once you are open for business). I usually recommend that you look at the typical Cash Flow Statement for a Business Plan and use it as a guide to estimate the costs for starting and operating your business. Start gathering these costs now so you can include them in the Business Plan. Include every possible expenditure you may incur from advertising to build-out of a new facility.

- The third area is Funding. Although we will address this in more detail in Stage IV - Funding, suffice it to say that it is never too early to start investigating the options that are available. Understanding the funding needs and the source of financing will be a critical step in the launch of your business. Being under-capitalized is one of the primary reasons for small business failures. Consider:

  - Personal investment: Whether you expect to get an investor, bank loan or money from friends and family you should still make a personal investment into the business. In fact, most banks or investors will expect you to invest some of your own money in the business. They call it "having 'skin' in the game".

- Friends and Family: Obtaining capital from your friends and family is certainly a viable option. However, you must weigh the risk of losing those funds (and the subsequent strain it will place on your relationships) against the reward of the business becoming the success you think it will become.

- Bank Loans: Banks obviously do make loans. They make their profit from the interest on those loans, but even more so from the fees and charges they collect from their depositors. Not all banks make loans for start-up ventures. It is just too risky for them. Remember that they make LOANS. They are not INVESTORS willing to lose their money. In fact, they are very insistent that you pay them back! Do your homework on which banks are lending to start-up ventures. Not all a banks lend to all clients.

- Lines of Credit: Lenders will often extend lines of credit to their business banking customers for the purchase of inventory or for special cash requirements. Discuss this option with your banker. It may enable you to obtain a smaller loan and supplement it with the line of credit.

- Credit cards: In the absence of other means of obtaining capital, many entrepreneurs are turning to credit cards as a financing option. Although they do represent a source of capital, it is very easy to run up bills with little or no ability to fulfill your financial obligation to the credit card company. And, the interest rates can be very high as well.

- Crowdfunding: This approach lets inventors and product suppliers post their products online and obtain pledges for product sales prior to actually going into production. It allows the inventor to gage (unscientifically) the interest in the product before sinking a lot of money in the project. On the downside, it also exposes the product to the public giving possible competitors with deeper pockets an opportunity to enter the market first. The concept is popular with music, film and literary developers. According to Wikipedia, the United States based company ArtistShare (2000/2001) is documented as being the first crowdfunding website for music followed later by sites such as Sellaband (2006), Indiegogo (2008), Pledge Music (2009), Kickstarter (2009), RocketHub (2009), InvestedIn (2010), GoFundMe (2010), Earlyshares (2011), Rock The Post (2011), Helpersunite (2011) and in the UK Sponsume (2010) and PleaseFund.Us (2011), Peerbackers (2008), Peoplefund.it (2012) and Fundable (2012).

- Grants: Many prospective entrepreneurs hang their hopes on obtaining a grant to fund their business. Be very careful of those who promote grants to start-up and expand your small business. For information on government grants go to www.grants.gov. In fact, the SBA makes it clear that they do NOT offer grants for small businesses. The following is a quote from the SBA website: *"Please note that SBA does not offer grants to start or expand small businesses. Those grant programs that SBA does offer are primarily designed to expand and enhance organizations that provide small business management, technical, or financial assistance."* www.SBA.gov

- And finally, the Financial Summary. To determine whether your business venture is feasible from a financial perspective prepare the following documents:

- General Assumptions: List any assumptions that were made which affect your financial projections

- Start-up Costs: List all the start-up costs

- Pre-Launch Income: List all possible pre-launch income from investments, loans or other sources

- Pricing/Projections: List proposed price per unit, Cost of Goods Sold (COGS) and projected unit sales per month

- Complete a Cash Flow projection (3 years)

- Complete a Balance Sheet

- Complete an Income Statement
  The Bottom Line: Identify the funding sources for your business and determine the requirements for obtaining the financing.

Measurement/Milestones

How will the success of the venture be evaluated and measured? What milestones need to be met in order to accomplish the objectives as a company and within each department?

An entrepreneur should realize that as an owner, there are a number of criteria by which you are expected to measure success. And while Sales is certainly one of them, it is not the only factor. Each department within a company should establish the criteria by which its individual success will be measured, especially in relation to the other departments and the company as a whole. The department's success is tied to the company's success and that is where the entrepreneur comes in.

Begin by defining the vision and mission of the company in terms of objectives and milestones. What do you want the company to accomplish in 90 days, 1 year, three years...? The list could include items like gross sales, profitability, "employer of the year" awards, etc.

Now, what needs to happen, by whom and by what date in each department of the company (and ultimately by each employee of the company) to accomplish the overall vision of the entrepreneur and the Mission of the company?

Remember that ultimately, the company's Mission and Milestones should support your own personal Mission! As an action step, prepare a chart indicating the milestones you will target for launching and growing the venture. The manager of each department should be able to assist in this exercise. Identify:

1. Schedules
2. Budgets
3. Responsibility

Market Opportunity Matrix

Following is an example of a Marketing Opportunity Matrix which I use for my consulting business.

Market Segment	Segment A: Insurance Agencies	Segment B Restaurants	Segment C Energy Co.	Segment D Daycare	Segment E Landscape Companies
Motivation	Help their clients	Toughest Sm. Biz to keep afloat	Major market opp.	Small but need advice	Small but need advice
Market (Buyers)	Agency Clients	Restaurant owners	Owner	Owner	Owner
Market (Influencers)	Agency owner	Restaurant Customers	Customer churches	Customer churches	Customer churches
Market (Strategic Partners)	CPA's, Attorneys	Food/ vendor suppliers	Vendors, suppliers	Vendors, suppliers	Vendors, suppliers
Market (Organizations)	Chamber of Commerce, State Insurance Comm.	Chamber of Commerce Restaurant Assn.	Trade assn.	Network org.	Network org.
Market (Competitors)	XYZ Consultant	Restaurant consultant	Business consultant	Business consultant	Business consultant
Magic (Products)	Write business plans	Write business plans	Write business plans	Write business plans	Write business plans
Magic (Services)	Sm. Biz Coaching	Sm. Biz Coaching	Sm. Biz Coaching	Sm. Biz Coaching	Sm. Biz Coaching
Magic (Packages)	Sm. Biz Consult.	Sm. Biz Consult.	Sm. Biz Consult.	Sm. Biz Consult.	Sm. Biz Consult.
Mandatory's	Investigate Insurance license	None	None	Investigate Daycare license	None
Media	Trade Shows, Website	Trade Shows, Website	Trade Shows, Website	Trade Shows, Website	Trade Shows, Website

The Bottom Line...

Is your Concept feasible?

1. Have you identified and established the specific NEED your company will address? (Motivation)
2. Have you identified who has the need (Buyers) and how many there are - Target Market Size? (Market)
3. Have you described how you will meet the need? (Magic)
4. Have you identified the best model (franchise, business acquisition, start-from-scratch) for your business to meet the need? (Model)
5. Have you identified the Mandatory's (Permits, Licenses, certifications) that are required to meet the need? (Mandatory's)
6. Have you identified the media tools that are available to communicate your solution to those in need? (Media)
7. Have you identified the people necessary to establish and manage the company so that it can effectively meet the needs of your customers? (Management)
8. Have you identified the strategies you will use to meet the need? (Method)
   a. Marketing strategy
   b. Personnel strategy
   c. Production/Operations strategy
   d. Financing strategy
   e. Customer strategy
9. Have you identified the money necessary to start/sustain the business and whether there will be sufficient revenue to build a profitable business? (Money)

10. Have you established a schedule for developing and launching your business? (Measurement/Milestones)

If you cannot answer positively to each of these 10 questions, your idea may not be feasible. If not, go back and consider one of your other options.

Stage 3: Plan

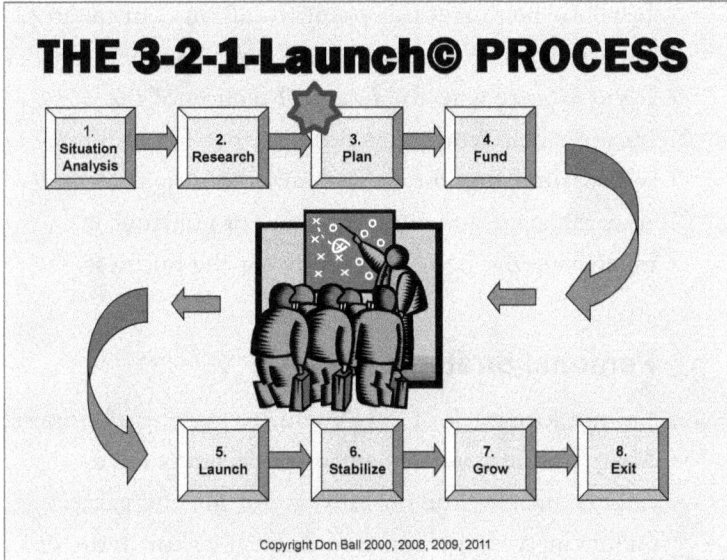

THE 3-2-1-Launch© PROCESS

| 1. Situation Analysis | 2. Research | 3. Plan | 4. Fund |

| 5. Launch | 6. Stabilize | 7. Grow | 8. Exit |

Copyright Don Ball 2000, 2008, 2009, 2011

Using the data, notes, and observations compiled during the last two stages (Stage I-Situation Analysis and Stage II-Feasibility Research) the objective of this stage is to assimilate all the information into two comprehensive plans: a Personal Strategic Plan and a Business Plan.

In the Personal Strategic Plan, you will present your personal vision for yourself and how the new business venture will help accomplish your goals. The Business Plan presents the method and organization (Management, Legal, Financial, Marketing, Sales, IT, HR, Customer Service and Operations) for how you plan to achieve the business success which will, in

97

turn, lead to the accomplishment of the Personal Strategic Plan.

It will be helpful at this point to call on your mentors for assistance. For instance, ask your Banker and CPA for assistance with the financial section of the business plan, your marketing partner for assistance with assimilating the data obtained during the research stage and your attorney for guidance in identifying the right legal entity for the business.

Personal Strategic Plan

Do not lose track of WHY you are starting a business. Many business owners and entrepreneurs fail to understand that the business is not the end game. Achieving your personal goals (in the short term and even when you stop working full-time) is the end game, and these goals are accomplished by establishing and operating a successful business.

Go back to Stage I-Situation Analysis and review the notes you made about your personal goals and objectives. Those notes tell you where you are now. A Personal Strategic Plan builds on that information to set a personal direction for you and your family.

Use the data you gathered in Stage I-Situation Analysis to develop a formal, written Personal Strategic Plan focused on the following areas:

- Your SWOT's: Restate your Strengths, Weaknesses, and the Opportunities and Threats you face. Beside each write a statement of how you will:
  - Expand on the Strengths
  - Allow for the Weaknesses
  - Capitalize on the Opportunities
  - Identify, anticipate and plan for the Threats
- Your Vision: (*Definition: An aspirational description of what you would like to achieve or accomplish in the mid-term or long-term future. It is intended to serve as a clear guide for choosing current and future courses of action. See also mission statement. Source: www.businessdictionary.com*) Someone once said that to accomplish a goal you must first envision the goal. In Stage I you captured information about WHERE YOU ARE NOW. This step calls for you to envision WHERE YOU WANT TO BE and gives you permission to dream a bit. Go back to the six items we addressed in Stage I-Situation Analysis, and envision what you want that area to become in the next 5-, 10-, and 15- years. Also, include your vision for age 60! (It comes a lot sooner than you may think!) For instance, what is your vision of:
  - Your Personal situation (i.e. Family, assets, etc.)
  - Your Employment situation (i.e. In control of my own employment situation)
  - Your Educational attainment (i.e. To obtain my Bachelor's degree)
  - Your Financial situation (i.e. To have a financial plan which will enable me to provide for my family now and after I'm gone)

- Your Physical situation (i.e. To get myself in better shape)
- Your Stakeholder situation (i.e. To identify and develop methods for improving my relationship with those who matter the most in my life)

Paint a big picture for yourself and your family of what you would like life to be like. It's obvious we cannot control world politics, the economy, and many other things. But given a perfect situation, what do you want for you and your family. This gets right to the core of who you are and what is important for you and your family. Consider things such as the ability to help others, provide a college education for your children (or grandchildren), or actively participate in a charitable or religious organization. It would be wise to have your family participate in this step. What is important to you may not be so critical to them. Remember, too, that this is not developing a "Wish List" of things you want (cars, houses, etc.). This step goes deeper into the things that would be important even if the business were NOT successful.

And that brings up a critical thought! Many think that the reason to have their own business is to have "things." Believe me, it is much more important to have values and dig deeper into what you will be able to accomplish if the business is successful.

Now, summarize all this into a paragraph called a "Vision Statement".

- Your Values for the business: (*Definition: In general, important and enduring beliefs or ideals shared by the members of a culture about what is good or desirable and what is not. Values exert major influence on the behavior of an individual and serve as broad guidelines in all situations. Source: www.businessdictionary.com*) This is a very personal step. It has to do with your standards and the "culture" for the business. Words and ideas like "Truth," "Honesty," and "Integrity" come to mind here. Establish some standards for how your business will be operated. Setting these standards before you start your business will provide you with benchmarks as you make decisions in the operation of your business.

- Goals and objectives: (*Definition: Summarized in the phrase "dream with a deadline," a goal is an observable and measurable end result having one or more objectives to be achieved within a more or less fixed timeframe. In comparison, a 'purpose' is an intention (internal motivational state) or mission. The question, "Has the goal been achieved?" can always be answered with either a "Yes" or "No." A purpose, however, is not 'achieved' but instead is pursued every day. Source: www.businessdictionary.com*) Next, determine the individual steps, the resources and the dates necessary to make each goal a reality. You cannot achieve what you cannot measure. Refer back to the Vision Statement and your Strengths and Weaknesses and list your personal goals and the dates by which you want to achieve them. Next, list the steps you will take to accomplish those goals. Is there training involved? Are there certifications you must obtain? Do you need to lose weight or set-up a savings account?

- "In 5 years I envision ... all my family being healthy, graduated from college and working in fulfilling positions." To achieve this goal I must…1….2…3… by (date).
- "In 10 years I envision...Having completed the degree I never finished." To achieve this goal I must…1….2…3… by (date).
- "In 15 years I envision...my wife and I taking a year off and living with a missionary in a foreign country." To achieve this goal I must…1….2…3… by (date).
- You get the idea.

The Bottom Line…

When you die, what legacy do you want to leave? (Definition: something handed down or received from an ancestor or predecessor. Source: www.thefreedictionary.com.) What words do you want others to use to define and describe your life?

It will be helpful to call on your Core Team to help with both the Personal Strategic Plan and the Business Plan. They are your advisors and can provide valuable insight into their specific areas of expertise.

The Business Plan

The Business Plan serves as a roadmap for the business. It presents the owner's ideas, concepts and dreams in a concise, focused document that a potential investor, potential employee or even a supplier can read to gain a better understanding of what the business is all about. There are five basic sections to a Business Plan: The Table of Contents; the Executive Summary; the Text, or Body, of the Plan; the Financial section; and the Exhibits or Attachments.

I have a client who has been working on a business idea for over five years. He felt that it was time to pull all the elements together and "make it happen." He is well known in his industry and has identified a worldwide network of distributors for his products as well as a key manufacturer to produce, package and ship his products. All he needed was...money! And in order to get money, he needed a business plan.

Not surprisingly, I suggested that he identify the key data (See Stage II- Feasibility Research) for the business plan so he could present a clear picture of his business and his financial needs to prospective investors.

He pulled a draft business plan from his briefcase and I agreed to read it and make comments. In the meantime (following a quick glance at the document during the meeting), I forwarded an outline for a "typical" business plan with instructions for what was to be included in each section.

The reading of his business plan was difficult at best. The author repeated himself, used different type fonts, underlined and bolded words in almost every paragraph. Not surprisingly, the page numbers didn't match the page listings in the Table of Contents.

I suggested that he rewrite the plan using the data he had included, but in the format and structure that I had provided to him. He spent hours revising the plan, but it was still disjointed and difficult to read. We spent our next 2-1/2 hour meeting going over each section of the plan to insure he really understood what was required.

What's the point of this example? Actually there are a couple of points:

- Writing a business plan is not as easy as one might think.
- This is where you may want to call on one or more of those Core Team partners we discussed in the last chapter to help you. Perhaps the CPA can help with the financials. The Marketing Specialist can assist with the strategic sections and the attorney and banker can assist with other technical and organizational details of the plan.

There are a number of very good business plan templates available - both on the internet and as software that you can purchase and basically "fill in the blanks." Start your business plan by reviewing each section and writing a single sentence which answers the question or provides the information for that section. Do not worry about completing every section before moving on to the next. Go through and address each section, then come back and add details to make your presentation more complete.

+++++++++++++++++++++++++++++++++++

Cover Page: The Cover Page should include a logo and simply state the company name, the author, date and contact information.

Confidentiality Page: The next page establishes the confidentiality of the document and the requirement that the reader acknowledges that the information provided in the plan is being made available to them with the understanding that it will be kept confidential. Here is a sample of what might be included on the Confidentiality Page:

"The undersigned reader acknowledges that the information provided by _____ in this business plan is confidential; therefore, reader agrees not to disc lose it without the express written permission of _____.

It is acknowledged by reader that information to be furnished in this business plan is in all respects confidential in nature, other than information which is in the public domain through other means and that any disclosure or use of same by reader, may cause serious harm or damage to _____.

Upon request, this document is to be immediately returned to _____. ____ Signature, _____ Name (typed or printed) _____ Date

This is a business plan. It does not imply an offering of securities."

☐

Table of Contents: This is always completed at the end - after the Business Plan, the Financials and

Executive Summary have been completed. Be sure the pages match the actual pages in the document!

Executive Summary: This section is written last as a SUMMARY of the entire business plan. Although it is written last, it is typically the first section that is read by a potential investor or lender. Essentially, it "summarizes" the major points of the entire plan. It can be challenging to write because it forces the business owner to present the major points in a very concise way to help the reader to come to a quick understanding of the overall plan. The Executive Summary briefly states what the company does and what financial results are expected if funding is obtained. If you are seeking funds, state the amount of the funds, from what sources and the method you plan for repaying/returning those funds. ☐

- Situation: In this section you want to answer the following questions: Why are you writing this Business Plan? What is your motivation? Do you see an opportunity or a problem that you feel you can address? If you are an existing business, this is where you would include the history of the business. Also include information on the following aspects of your business:

- Past Performance: If you are an existing business include information about the history of your business, such as when it was formed, how large it is, and data about its performance (especially financial) to date. Include information explaining how this new idea/product or service will enhance the company's performance, especially financially. If this is a new business, you do not include this section.

- Environmental Analysis: What is the "environment" in which your business will be operating? Go back to the "Mandatory's" section of your feasibility research to determine if there were specific requirements which should be included here. For instance, consider government regulations such as zoning and, if having access to a highly skilled workforce is important include the fact that there are people in the area where you are planning to set-up shop. The objective of this section is to show that you have considered all the elements of a successful business and they exist where you plan to launch your venture.

- Current business conditions: Describe whether your business will be selling to a National, Regional, or Local market and what the conditions are within that geographic area. If the area is very supportive of new businesses (perhaps the local business community provides tax incentives or has a major, unemployed workforce which can support your business), you will want to convince investors/lenders that you have done your research and know that the area is the right place to launch your business.

I once worked with a start-up whose owner was an inventor from Minnesota. He identified a small community in Central Texas as having a large, unemployed workforce which could provide the manufacturing and assembly labor he needed to launch a new product. In his case there was added incentive to launch the business in this particular area because the state provided Economic Development funds to put the local job market to work.

The following sections make up the "Body" of the Business Plan. You will note that the data for each section comes from the research which was compiled in Section II: Feasibility Research.

Section 1: Motivation: This section will answer the following questions: What is the client's motivation for buying your product/service? What need will your product/service address? Is it a real or perceived need? What value does your product/service bring to the buyer? What has the marketplace used in the past?

Section 2: Market: It is important to display proof that you have researched your potential market thoroughly. Bankers and investors want to know that you know who the buyers are, how many there are and you know exactly how you will go about convincing them your product or service is superior to any other product on the market.

Start by presenting a Market Analysis that describes the market for your products and services. You compiled this information during the Stage II: Feasibility Research phase. Begin by inserting a brief overview of the specific industry description here.

As you recall, each business is in a Standard Industrial Classification (SIC) or, as it is now known, North American Industry Classification System (NAICS). (If you are not sure of your classification code go to: http://www.census.gov/eos/www/naics/ and enter in your business type. For instance, if you are starting a full-service restaurant you are in NAICS Code no. 722110, "Restaurants, Full Service." If you are selling restaurant furniture you are in NAICS Code No. 337127, "Restaurant Furniture."

• Identify the potential MARKET SEGMENTS you have selected to sell your products into.
• Describe/profile the BUYERS to whom you will be selling within each market segment including information such as the geographical area in which your buyers can be found, the buying capacity (their ability to actually afford your product/service), and their need for your products (does your product respond to a real or perceived need?)
• Describe/profile the INFLUENCERS who can impact the buyers' decision to acquire your product/service.
• Describe/profile the STRATEGIC PARTNERS whom you can work with to reach the Buyers and Influencers.
• Identify the ASSOCIATIONS, CHAMBERS and ORGANIZATIONS which you will become active in to reach your buyers.

You may be able to present the target market information in a table format such as:

TARGET MARKET NAME	Total Market Size (5 Mi. Radius)	Yr. 1 Target %	Yr. 1 Target No. (Tot. Mkt. X %)	Typical Unit Sales Value	Annual Value of Sales to Market Segment
Insurance Agencies	23	20	4.6	$ 5,236	$ 24,085
Restaurants	75	7	5.25	$ 1,429	$ 7,502.25
Energy Companies	6	50	3	$ 13,980	$ 41,940.00
Daycares	12	25	3	$ 523	$ 1,569.00
Landscape Companies	17	10	1.7	$ 126	$ 214.20

- **Competitive Analysis:** Define and give examples of your competition. You identified some of them in the Feasibility Research section, so this should not be a problem for you. Remember that a "Competitor" is typically defined as "any alternative to your solution." Competitors will probably have the same NAICS code as your business and are located or operating in the same geographical area. Lenders and investors want to know that you have done your research about the competition. Include the following information, perhaps in a matrix format, about your competitors:

Competitor	No. Offices	Gross Sales	Strengths	Weaknesses	Notes
Competitor A	6	$1.8M	Stability	Old technology	Possible acquisition candidate
Competitor B	1	$250K	Solid	Not growth oriented	Consider
Competitor C	17	$7.3M	Cash strong	Resources leveraged	Do not consider
Competitor D	25	$14.8M	Mgmt. Team	PR Issues	Low prospects
Competitor E	12	$13.0M	Multi-Natl.	Lost CEO	Good candidate

Section 3: Magic: Explain the products and services you have to offer each market segment? Clearly define each major product, describing each in terms of price, features, benefits, production time, COGs %, etc. Also, include information about any legal protection that might be required for the product (Trademark, Copyright, and Patent) and at what cost? Also indicate whether you will require a prototype and, if so, how you plan to produce it and at what cost?

Section 4: Model: Explain the business model will you use? (Franchise, standalone retail, manufacturer, distributor, web sales, affiliate marketing web sales, etc.) Indicate the legal structure for the business (Sole Proprietor, LLC, S-Corp., etc.)

☐

Section 5: Mandatories: It is important to state the requirements that must be met before you can start selling? You should have identified these requirements in Stage II: Feasibility Research. Indicate any permits, licenses, certificates, etc. that is necessary and the status in obtaining those permits and licenses.
☐

Section 6: Media: It is important to detail how you plan to "market" your Company, your Brand and your Products and Services. Identify the Media tools available to promote the products/services, such as a website, trade show booth, yellow page ad, brochure, uniforms, etc. and which of them (or a combination of them) are most appropriate to promote your venture. It is helpful to include the rates for each media tool as well.

Section 7: Management: Identify the key people who will insure the success of the business and include a brief (1 paragraph) bio for each. Include a resume in the Appendix to provide more information. You might want to divide this section into Mentors, Key managers, Staff:

- Mentors: Identify the key individuals who will serve on your Advisory Board
- Key Managers: Prepare an organization chart and identify the professionals you will hire to manage each department-whether internal or on an outsource basis (Sales, Marketing, Finance, Legal, HR, IT, Customer Service and Operations/Production))
- President: (Name) (Bio, resume in the exhibits section)

- Admin: (Name) (Bio, resume in the exhibits section)
- Sales (Name) (Bio, resume in the exhibits section)
- Marketing (Name) (Bio, resume in the exhibits section)
- Finance (Name) (Bio, resume in the exhibits section)
- Legal (Name) (Bio, resume in the exhibits section)
- HR (Name) (Bio, resume in the exhibits section)
- IT (Name) (Bio, resume in the exhibits section)
- Customer Service (Name) (Bio, resume in the exhibits section)
- Operations (Name) (Bio, resume in the exhibits section)

- Staff: If space will allow, and these people are very important to the success of your venture, include information about those who will serve under these managers and what explain their job functions? It is not necessary to include Job Descriptions in the Business Plan, but indicate that they are available.
- Competition: Research how your competition is organized. It may give you some hints on what you should do, and what NOT, to do.

Section 8: Method (Strategies): Identify the proposed strategies for the following :)
- Marketing Strategy: Using the data collected during the Stage II-Feasibility Research, describe how you plan to reach your target market with your primary message. Start by defining the target market, and then present your Value Statement and Unique Sales Proposition-USP (what differentiates you/your products/services from the competition). Include information on Promotion, Position, Pricing,

Production and Distribution. For instance, will you target families or corporations? While you might have a larger market in families, you may be able to gain sales faster by going to corporations and then selling to the families of the employees who work there.

- Competitive strategy: Describe how you will position your Company/Brand/Products and Services against those of your competition. Words like "Faster", "Closer", Free Delivery", etc. help to position your company's strengths against your competitors' weaknesses. How

- Personnel strategy: Explain your Personnel strategy in terms of the types of people you will bring on board. Are you hiring minimum wage staff, or will your company require C-level people to insure its success? Explaining the personnel strategy here will be important when a banker sees very high salaries in the financial section!

- Operations and Production strategy: How do you plan to produce your product or service? Based on your extensive research you should be able to explain that the company will manufacture all its key components in-house, but that some critical items will be acquired from a third party and all assembly work will be done in-house. It is important to show that you have redundancies in place in the event that a key supplier is unable to deliver critical components on time. This section presents your methods and plans for actually producing your products and services. Include information on production capacity, costs and inventory controls, and how you plan to invoice and collect receivables. Also include a section on personnel (how they will be selected, trained and evaluated) You do not have to include an organization chart, but give enough information to convince the reader you know exactly how many employees you will need, when you will hire them and your philosophy on compensating them.

- Financing strategy: In this section explain how you plan to finance this venture. You may be seeking Venture Capital money, an SBA-guaranteed loan or simply a line of credit-or even some combination of all three. Be as specific as possible because this section sends a message to your funders as to how they should look at your deal and how they will benefit from working with you.
  ☐

Section 9: Milestones: What are the major milestones you must accomplish in launching your product development, sales, marketing and production initiatives? Prepare a chart indicating the key dates for launching and growing the venture. Also include Budgets and who has responsibility for each aspect of the launch. The manager of each department should be able to assist in this exercise. ☐

Section 10: Measurement: What criteria will you use to measure the success of your sales and marketing program? For instance, success can be measured based on Sales numbers, financial goals and even results from customer surveys.

Section 11: Money: This is perhaps the most critical part of your business plan. It will state in financial terms what you plan to do with the money you are seeking, how much money you anticipate making (Revenue) each month and how much you anticipate spending (Expenses) each month. It will also provide ratios that compare your financial position to others in like businesses. You will also answer the question that banks always want to know: "How much are you willing to invest to insure the success of your business venture?"

Some of the specific aspects of this section include:

- General Assumptions: List any assumptions that were made which affect your financial projections. Explain how you developed the numbers in the financial section. Establish the rationale behind each of the following: revenue, costs and expenses. Providing clear explanations assures greater credibility for your plan in the eyes of an investor. This section should not be difficult to prepare as you have established many of the "Assumptions" as you were conducting your Feasibility Research. Stating the assumptions helps to establish the credibility for your plan.
- Revenue Streams: Go back to Section 3: Magic to identify all the revenue streams which the company can pursue?.
- Pricing/projections: List proposed price per unit, COGS, and projected unit sales per month for each product.
- Pre-launch Income: List all possible pre-launch income from investments, loans, lines of credit, equity investors, and even friends and family.

- Start-up costs: List all the start-up costs you identified in the Stage II. Feasibility Research phase.
- Complete a Cash Flow projection (3 years) based on the data you developed in the Stage II. Feasibility Research phase. In any business "Cash is King." If you cannot pay the bills you will not have a business for long. Based on the assumptions you stated at the beginning of the Financial Section, present the "flow of cash" on a monthly basis. It is set-up much like your check book in that you have the starting balance for each month and then you include the revenue you will generate (Gross Income), minus the cost of the goods sold (COGS) which results in your net income. Below this section are your projected expenses for the month (rent, payroll, advertising, loan payments, etc.). The bottom line (literally) is what you will have at the end of the month (which will go to the top of the next month's cash flow projection). If you end up with a negative for the month, you must make adjustments - either find additional revenue (increase sales) or decrease expenses.

Be careful that you are not overly optimistic in your sales forecasts! Lenders and investors will scrutinize your cash flow forecast to insure that you will be able to cover loan payments, interest and taxes. A tip to remember: Do not estimate your annual sales projections and then divide by 12 to get a monthly revenue forecast. This is a major "red flag" indicating that you have no idea how your sales will start and grow over time.

By identifying the net cash results each month an entrepreneur will be able to determine the amount of funds that will be necessary to keep the business solvent and when the business will be able to stand on its own. Asking for too much or too little cash and at the wrong times can send signals to your lenders that you do not really understand how cash will flow through your business. Knowing exactly what you need and when you need it helps prove that you have done your homework.

Like the other financial forecast statements, your Cash Flow Forecast should be shown on a monthly basis covering a three year period.

- Complete a Balance Sheet based on the data you developed in the Stage II. Feasibility Research phase. The balance sheet shows what the business owns and what the business owes to others and to its owners. The two must "balance." Balance sheets are typically prepared on a monthly basis for the first year and quarterly for the next two years.

- Complete an Income Statement based on the data you developed in the Stage II. Feasibility Research phase. Income statements are simply a projection of your Profit & Loss based on the assumptions you identified at the beginning of this section. Although some lenders will only require a two-year forecast, others want a three-year projection. So, project out three years just to be safe. They know that there are many factors that make the third year of projections less certain.

- Key Ratios: Lenders need some measure to compare your financial projections against in order to determine if your business premise is viable. They use "Key Ratios" as their standard. Each industry has its own set of key ratios and a lender will pull this data and compare against your ratios to see how you compare to others in your industry. Trade Associations, banks and other financial sources can provide the standard key ratios for your industry.

- Other items: Be prepared to provide a personal financial statement for lenders and investors. They look at the personal financials to understand how you have handled your personal finances and to anticipate how you will handle their money. Also, be prepared to present details of how you will use the funds they are providing.

- **Exhibits:** In this section include items that will further support some statement or section of the business plan. Do not clutter the plan with a lot of data which will not add to the reader's understanding or further justify a portion of the plan.

For instance, if you state that the business has been incorporated, the lender will assume you have the paperwork to back up your claim. You can present it if requested, but you do not have to include it in the Exhibits section.

The Bottom line...

Prepare a Personal Strategic Plan to establish why you are even starting a business and how you perceive that by having the business you will be able to accomplish those personal objectives. Then prepare a written Business Plan to present to possible lenders/investors as well other stakeholders, which indicate you, have done your homework and are prepared to launch a successful business, based on solid research and investigation. You do not just "THINK" the business will be successful, you "KNOW" the business will be successful!

Stage 4: Fund

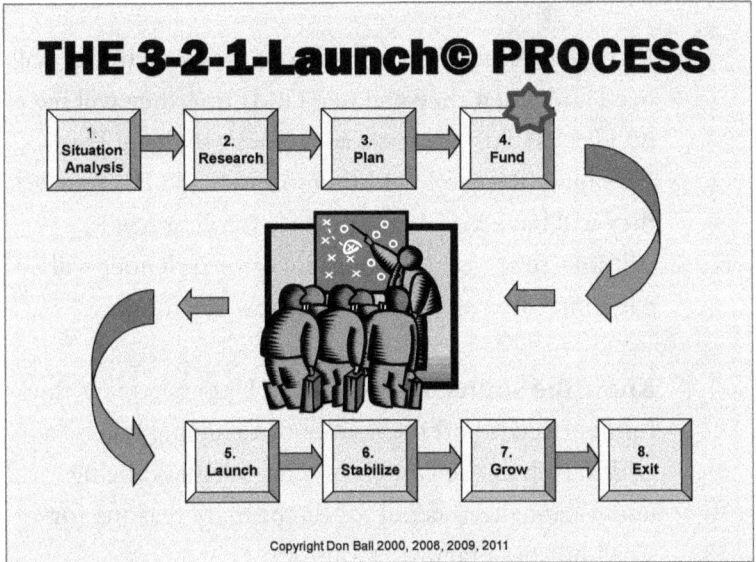

THE 3-2-1-Launch© PROCESS

| 1. Situation Analysis | 2. Research | 3. Plan | 4. Fund |
| 5. Launch | 6. Stabilize | 7. Grow | 8. Exit |

Copyright Don Ball 2000, 2008, 2009, 2011

Introduction: Obtaining the necessary funds for launching and sustaining your business venture is based on three critical components: knowing how much you will need; knowing the source of the funds; and, knowing and meeting the requirements for obtaining those funds.

Knowing how much you will need: The data developed during Stage II-Feasibility Research and Stage III-Plan is critical to knowing how much capital you will need to start and sustain your business. Quite often I ask my new clients how much money they think they will need to start and launch a successful business. Some answer quickly with an estimate while others admit they have no idea. The next question I ask is very telling - "Have you written a Business Plan?"

If so, they should have an idea of how much they will need and when they will need it. If not, they will have no idea. At this point we move back to Stage II-Feasibility Research and then on to Stage III-Plan, so they will have a real idea of their funding needs. Without firm, solid data, no investor or lender will pay much attention to your request for funding.

Know the source of the funds: Understanding the funding needs and the source of financing will be a critical step in the launch of your business. Being under-capitalized is one of the primary reasons for small business failures. Consider:

- Personal investment: Whether you expect to get an investor, bank loan or money from friends and family you should still make some personal investment into the business. In fact, most banks or investors expect you to invest some of your own money in the business. As stated earlier, we call this "having 'skin' in the game".

- Friends and Family: Obtaining capital from your friends and family is certainly a viable option. However, one should consider the risks along with the rewards. Let's presume you have received money from Mom, Dad, Grandma, your in-laws and your brother-in-law. Wow, you think, these people all believe in my idea and are willing to support my dream. What an endorsement! But do not forget that next Thanksgiving you will be sitting down at the table with not only friends and family, but also your investors. Although it may go unsaid, the question of how well their investment is performing will always be in the back of their minds. You are having Thanksgiving Dinner with friends, family and investors. Keep this in mind when you accept their check!

- Bank Loans: While these are certainly a major method for small businesses to consider, the number of banks that are actually making loans for start-up businesses has been dropping due to tough economic times. Each lender will scrutinize your business plan and assess your ability to repay very carefully.

  In fact, when one bank president was asked if his bank was making loans for start-ups, he assured that they were, "as long as they can show us two years of financials." That is not a start-up.

- Lines of Credit: Just like the credit limit extended by a credit card company, a line of credit (also called a credit line or credit limit) is the maximum amount of money a lender will extend to a business or individual without requiring any additional credit approval. The primary difference is the interest rate charged for the loan. Businesses typically use lines of credit for purchasing inventory and other capital expenditures. Although the bank may extend a $10,000 line of credit, the business owner may take out smaller amounts up to that maximum amount with the idea that interest rates may (probably will) change; therefore, they may only take out the amount they have an immediate need for.

- Credit cards: In the absence of other means of obtaining capital, some entrepreneurs are turning to credit cards as a financing option. A word of caution. These credit cards typically carry very high interest rates. Just because they offer a high "credit line" doesn't mean it is the best option. If you can't pay it back before the high interest rate kicks in, it may be a better option to consider other means for capital.

- Crowdfunding: Wikipedia defines Crowdfunding as: Crowd funding or crowdfunding (alternately crowd financing, equity crowdfunding, or hyper funding) describes the collective effort of individuals who network and pool their resources, usually via the Internet, to support efforts initiated by other people or organizations. Crowd funding can also refer to the funding of a company by selling small amounts of equity to many investors.

Crowd funding is used in support of a wide variety of activities, including disaster relief, citizen journalism, support of artists by fans, political campaigns, Startup Company funding, movie or free software development, inventions development and scientific research.
(http://en.wikipedia.org/wiki/Crowd_funding) Some of the popular Crowdfunding sites include:

Kickstarter (2009), RocketHub (2009), InvestedIn (2010), and GoFundMe (2010).

- Grants: Many prospective entrepreneurs hang their hopes on obtaining a grant to fund their business. Be very careful of the promotion of grants to start-up and expand your small business. For information on government grants go to www.grants.gov. In addition, for a good site regarding grant opportunities from Foundations and Corporations visit www.fundsnetservices.com.

I think it is worth repeating what we said earlier about the SBA's position regarding grants. Following is a quote from the SBA website:

"Please note that SBA does not offer grants to start or expand small businesses. Those grant programs that SBA does offer are primarily designed to expand and enhance organizations that provide small business management, technical, or financial assistance." www.SBA.gov

To learn what, if any, grants you might qualify for, complete the Grants and Loans questionnaire (www.business.gov)

Know and meet the requirements to obtain the funds: Getting a loan is not an easy task. Lenders are taking a risk that you will pay the money back. The more defaults they experience in a year, the more carefully they will scrutinize your situation.

When approaching a lender take an A, B, C's approach:

A- What is your **A**ttitude? Are you really passionate about your business idea?

B- Do you have a **B**usiness Plan? If not, go back to Stage II-Feasibility Research, conduct your research, then write a solid, well thought-out Business Plan (Stage III-Plan).

C- What is your **C**redit score? Lenders will look at credit reports to determine your past history of handling money and credit and to determine your ability to repay the loan.

D- Can you pay the **D**eposit? Lenders require, typically, anywhere from 10%-30% from the borrower to make a loan. The deposit amount is determined on a case by case basis and varies from lender to lender.

E- What is your **E**xperience? They want to know that you have actual, hands-on experience in the business you are about to launch. Enjoying food is not adequate experience to obtain funding for a restaurant!

As you can see, obtaining funds is not an easy task!

The Bottom Line...

Do your homework before you go to a lender or find a partner and think through the consequences and responsibilities of obtaining a loan for your business.

Stage 5: Launch

THE 3-2-1-Launch© PROCESS

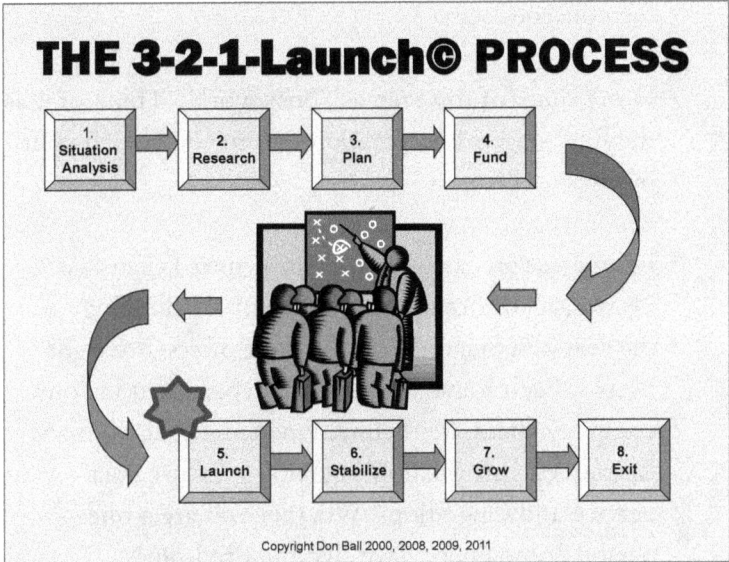

| 1. Situation Analysis | 2. Research | 3. Plan | 4. Fund |

| 5. Launch | 6. Stabilize | 7. Grow | 8. Exit |

Copyright Don Ball 2000, 2008, 2009, 2011

Once an entrepreneur "gets the money" they often feel like they have reached the summit. They have a bank account that was stocked by someone else (a bank or investor) who believed in them. So, now what?

Entrepreneurs should take the time to adequately prepare _**before**_ launching their business. In this stage we will discuss three primary steps to insure that the business is established on a solid foundation: Pre-launch, Soft Launch and Launch. Some entrepreneurs skip this step and just throw the doors open and scream, "We're open for business!" Unfortunately, without addressing the steps outlined in this stage, they may find themselves floundering as they proceed with their business, making decisions on the fly without giving adequate thought and consideration to the consequences.

Don't think of this step as "busy work". Think of it as the final stage of preparation before you launch your business.

Let me use an example, well known to Texans. As Owner of your own company think of climbing on the seat of a Stage Coach. In front of you are eight horses. Each horse represents a department in your company: Sales, Marketing, Finance, Legal, Human Resources, Information Technology, Customer Service and Operations. Whether you are a one-person company or have five-hundred-plus employees, the basic department break-down is the same. The only difference is that in a one-person operation, at least to start, YOU, the owner, are also the Marketing Manager, the Sales Manager, the Operations guy...etc.

Not surprisingly, entrepreneurs are most familiar with Operations. This is the area which will produce whatever it is your company will sell. If you are a writer, you "produce" written pieces. If you are opening a sandwich shop, you "produce" sandwiches. If you are in Lawn Care, you mow, trim, blow and bag. While there is no doubt Operations is critical to the success of your business, so is Sales...and Marketing...and Human Resources...etc.

Back to our Stage Coach analogy… I've seen many entrepreneurs start-off riding on the seat of their coach, holding the reins and in control of the business, only to find them in a month or two…when things start getting tough…climbing down on one of the horses and focusing on Sales, or Marketing or, as is usually the case, riding the Operations horse. They usually gravitate to the area in which they are most comfortable. As a result, they are riding one of the eight horses and there are seven horses running wild. They've just lost control of their business!

The entrepreneur must always remind themselves that they are responsible for the Vision, the Direction and the Guidance for the business. To do that requires a different perspective on your business... a view from above - from the seat of the stage coach, not riding one of the horses. It is critical, therefore, to establish certain guidelines which will enable the owner to keep their eye on the future and the surroundings without becoming bogged down in the specifics of each department of the business.

Let me make it clear, however, that in the beginning, the Entrepreneur/Owner typically does everything. But your goal should be to organize and manage each function so that you can focus on the long-term vision for the company rather than the day to day details.

For instance, a small business owner who makes sandwiches knows that he also needs to compute and submit taxes on a quarterly basis. If the entrepreneur has the skills to do so, fine. If not, it may be a better use of time to hire an accountant or CPA to handle this function. This will free you up to do other things (like develop a new marketing campaign or negotiate a lower interest rate on a line of credit)—namely the things that only you can do. But, the owner needs to remember that they are ultimately responsible for the taxes, regardless of who is preparing them. You will have to sign the documents and answer questions if the IRS comes to discuss a discrepancy in the numbers.

Pre-launch

This step requires that you start looking inward at your business. Develop a written Strategic Operations Plan for the company and a separate Strategic Operations Plan for each Department. Notice that the plans include some of the same components of the Personal Strategic Plan you developed in Stage III-Plan. You are just applying those principles to your business.

Each department is responsible for developing its own Strategic Operations Plan which supports the Company's Strategic Operations Plan. The bottom line here is that the owner establishes and communicates the vision and direction for the business and each department develops the strategies to help the company reach its goals. This is a prime example of each player doing their part to help the team reach its goal.

There are objectives along the way that, when accomplished, add up to a "win". Everyone has to do their part to accomplish the win, and the owner must establish, and then monitor their performance to insure that everyone is running the same way. You, Mr. /Ms. Entrepreneur, are driving the stage coach and all the horses trust you to get them to the right location at the end of the trip. In addition, you should not forget that there are stakeholders riding in the coach who have certain expectations of you as well!

Following is a typical outline for each plan.

- **Company Strategic Operations Plan**
  - Situation (SWOT): Identify the Strengths, Weaknesses, Opportunities and Threats facing the company.
  - Vision Statement: Describe the business in three years in terms of physical appearance, size, etc.
  - Mission Statement: Define the purpose of the business ("To design, produce and deliver specific products for specific people via specific distribution methods").
  - Corporate Values: What values will the company follow with regard to how it will operate and interact with others (clients, employees, shareholders, community, etc.)?
  - Business Objectives: Establish the specific results which the company will achieve in one to three years.

131

- Key Strategies: Establish the rules and guidelines by which the Business Objectives will be achieved (i.e., Growth will be funded through internal cash flow).
- Major Goals: Identify specific milestones to be accomplished by implementing the strategies in pursuit of the company's objectives. Goals should be measureable, realistic and achievable.
- Strategic Action Programs: Describe the programs/projects that will be implemented to accomplish the company's business goals. The programs address the resources, objectives, deadlines, budgets and key performance indicators (KPI's) which will be used to measure success.
- Management Reports: Identify and describe the reports about the business which the Owner will prepare and submit to the stakeholders and on what schedule.

- **Strategic Operations Plan-Department:** The Owner presents the Company Strategic Operations Plan to the Department Managers so they can develop their specific Department Strategic Operations Plan to help meet the Company objectives.
  - Plan:
    - SWOT's: Identify the Strengths, Weaknesses, Opportunities and Threats of the Department
    - Vision: Describe the department in terms of what it will be doing in three years to

help accomplish the mission of the company as a whole

- Mission Statement: Describe the mission of the Department. For instance the Marketing Department might identify the following as its primary mission:
    - Insure methods are in place to assure the highest Customer Satisfaction
    - Conduct and analyze market research
    - Develop marketing strategies
    - Develop and implement marketing plan
    - Manage the corporate Brand
    - Provide department organizational management and leadership
- Corporate Values: Restate the Corporate values and how the Department will portray those Values. Again, the Marketing Department might use the following:
    - Communicate regularly with Management and other departments
    - Monitor, measure and report on KPI's
    - Support corporate mission
- Business Objectives: Describe the specific objectives for the Department in terms of the SWOT's. How will the Department

enhance its Strengths, compensate for its Weaknesses, capitalize on its Opportunities, and mitigate any Threats to the Department's success.

- Key Strategies: Describe the major strategies for the Department. The Marketing Department might use the following:
  - Strategy 1: Marketing Plan
  - Strategy 2: On-going Competitive research
- Major Goals: Identify the major goals the Department will achieve each year for the next three years. The Marketing Department might identify the following as Major Goals:
  - Goal 1:Create, position and maintain a positive Brand in the marketplace
  - Goal 2: Develop methods and monitor competitive activity in the marketplace

While the Strategic Operations Plan for each department presents WHAT it will accomplish, the Department Strategic Action Programs describe HOW it will be accomplished.

- **Department Strategic Action Programs**
  - Functions: Identify the primary functions of the Department, who will be responsible for that step, when it will be accomplished and at what expense. The functions are developed by the

Department Manager with final approval by the Entrepreneur. Functions include:

- Processes: What are the processes which the Department must follow? For instance, if you are making cheeseburgers there is a process for "building" a cheeseburger. Granted the customer can request that there be changes to the basic cheeseburger, but you need to have a standard by which to gage the performance and quality of the Cheeseburger. If the Cheeseburger is "built" without the cheese, the expectations of the customer are not met, inventory is affected, and human resources are impacted by an employee who does not follow the process. (It's important to manage the Process, not the employee.) Determine if the employee was attempting to follow the process, or just ignored it. If they ignored it and don't give any indication that they intend to follow the process, there may be grounds for termination-after having followed the proper process for reprimanding an employee! If the employee DID follow the process and the customer is unhappy, perhaps the Process needs to be changed.

- Personnel: Identify the right people to accomplish the tasks. Hiring your brother-in-law just because he has a truck to deliver mulch for your lawn care business is okay for a while, but your brother-in-law may not be willing to follow the "processes" you as the Owner have established for your business. This can make his employment tenuous and put your management of the company in jeopardy-especially in the eyes of other employees. Before hiring anyone the owner must insure they have the Processes and Job Descriptions for each person written down and that each employee is properly trained in the personnel policies and the KPI's.

- Training: Identify the training needs for everyone in each department from the Department Manager on down. Training on a regular basis shows the owner has a real desire to improve the performance and enhance the careers of each employee. Employees need to be exposed to the latest techniques for performing their duties. Providing training is often a good way to attract and retain employees. Training is critical regarding safety issues.

- Technology: Identify the technology needs for each department. It is critical that the needs be identified and addressed by the IT department so that each department can "talk" to one another. Communication is critical among employees, from the company to clients and with stakeholders. Be sure you have one person/department who will manage this function.

- Budget: Ah, the budget. You'll probably remember the agony you went through developing the financial section of the Business Plan and then to present the "budget" for the company to your financial partners. Now, you get to divide those dollars among your Departments. Make it clear that you will be monitoring their performance against the budget they have been assigned (and which was essentially approved by the bank when you received your loan!).

- KPI's: Key Performance Indicators are one of the most critical requirements an Owner must address to "stay in the seat" of the stage coach. Establish the metrics which you will use to monitor the performance of each department. The idea is to identify those areas that, if the department is meeting their KPI's, the company as a whole will meet its performance objectives. For instance, if the Marketing Department is charged with developing and launching a new website to promote your new product line, and they do not meet the due date, the sales department will be impacted because they are projecting revenue from sales. The human resource department will be impacted because they hired and trained new employees to be ready for the launch. You, as the Owner, must monitor the KPI's for each department to insure that everyone is still moving forward, to the same goal, at the same speed and on the same schedule. A horse that wants to walk when every other horse is running at full speed is going to impact the success of the company as a whole.

- Tasks: List the primary tasks for the department. For instance, the Marketing Department may be responsible for:
  - Marketing Plan
  - Identifying and hiring the creative staff
  - Identifying and monitoring the pricing for the product
  - Establishing the product distribution methods
  - Developing and implementing a method for monitoring competitive activities (Consider Google Alerts® to be notified on a daily basis of any news articles about your competitors)

Department Action Steps

Following are some examples of the department structures:

- **Management**
    - Management's Mission is to:
        - Insure methods are in place to assure the highest Customer Satisfaction
        - Develop, present and communicate corporate vision
        - Establish and support corporate culture
        - Provide leadership (Focus, Objectives, and encourage corporate and individual accomplishment)
        - Monitor Corporate performance
        - Monitor Department performance
        - Act on leadership responsibilities

    - Update _Corporate_ Strategic Operations Plan (Based on funding situation) focusing on: SWOT's, Vision, Mission Statement, Corporate Values, Business Objectives, Key Strategies, Major Goals, and Strategic Action Programs

    - Prepare and Implement _Department_ Strategic Operations Plans. These will be prepared by each department manager with the oversight of the Owner. The department Standard Operating Plan should include the following: SWOT's, Vision, Mission Statement,

139

Corporate Values, Business Objectives, Key
Strategies, Major Goals, and,, Strategic Action
Program.

- Focus on Department Functions. There are
  Functions that are common to each
  Department such as: Processes, Personnel,
  Training, Budgets, Technology, Deliverables
  (KPI's), and Management Reports.

  - Department Strategic Plan: The
    Owner will provide the outline and a
    copy of the Corporate Strategic
    Operations Plan so the Department
    Manager will know how his plan will
    relate to the overall scope of the
    business.

  - Processes: The Department Manager
    should list each of the processes for
    his department and who is responsible
    for monitoring performance against
    the process. Be specific with each
    process. This can be used as a part of
    the department orientation when you
    are adding a new employee. It also
    serves to accentuate how important
    each process is to the overall
    operations of the company.

  - Personnel: Prepare an organization
    chart for the department and indicate

what people you will need, with a job description, compensation and projected start-date. Provide a copy to the Human Resources Manager. Note that although the functions of this department may be outsourced for your business, especially in the early stages, management is still responsible for the results of this department's efforts.

- Training: Identify the training necessary for the department's employees. Indicate what type (supervisory, specific function, etc.), who will provide the training, when it will take place and the costs.

- Technology: Identify the technology needed for the department and the function the technology will serve. Submit the list to the IT department and allow them the ability to evaluate all department requests and make the purchase of hardware and software that will benefit the company as a whole and grow with the company. This is an example of when the Owner may have to serve as a mediator to insure that the department's needs are being met, while insuring there are some economies of scale. Try to keep personal preferences out of the equation.

- Budget: Prepare a detailed budget for the department. List all expenses and the dates for those expenses on a separate sheet. Next, provide the justification for each major expenditure. Be sure the department manager includes how the expenditure will positively impact the bottom line.

- Deliverables/KPI's: It is important that the Owner work closely with the Department Manager to identify the Key Performance Indicators (KPI's) which the owner will use to monitor the performance of the department. Areas which could be monitored include: movement toward accomplishment of specific department goals and objectives, the departments' adherence to processes, discussion of customer complaints/accolades, etc.

- Management Reports: The Owner should advise the department manager that the KPI's will be reviewed on a regular schedule. In addition, other items should be submitted, usually in

142

writing, in a management report which could include items like: personnel-; budget-; and customer service issues.

- Focus on Department Tasks: Each department has specific actions they will be responsible for performing. As the business owner your job will be to insure that each Department functions properly, the costs are effective, efficient and in-concert with the other departments.

- Identify methods and procedures for monitoring the company's performance (on department and company basis) including processes and KPI's

- **Marketing Department:**
  - The Marketing Department's Mission is to:
    - Insure methods are in place to assure the highest Customer Satisfaction
    - Conduct and analyze market research
    - Develop marketing strategies
    - Develop and implement marketing plan
    - Manage the Corporate Brand
    - Provide department organizational management and leadership
    - Communicate regularly with Management and other departments
    - Monitor, measure and report on KPI's
    - Support Corporate Mission

- Functions: There are Functions that are common to each Department such as: Processes, Personnel, Training, Budgets, Technology, Deliverables (KPI's), and Management Reports. Each Department Manager should coordinate its functions with management and other department operations.

- Tasks:
    - Marketing Plan: A marketing plan is based on a years' program and typically consists of the following data: Executive Summary, Opportunity and Marketing Goals, Situation Analysis (Company, Customer, Competitor, Environment), SWOT Analysis, Market Segmentation, Marketing Strategies, Product, Price, Place (Distribution), Promotion, short and long-term projections, and Conclusion.

    - It should be reviewed on a quarterly basis with input from other departments to insure the company is on-target with its marketing efforts and agree to changes and alterations in the plans, goals and objectives.

    - Customers: Develop a method to profile customers by capturing data on: customer profiles (are they changing-if so, why?); customer demographics; customer psychographics; etc. Your customers are

144

the most important asset you have for
your business.

- Competitors: Develop methods for
monitoring competitor activity. Consider
using tools like Google Alerts® to
maintain a daily "eye" on the competition.
Note any changes in their activity, pricing,
personnel additions/reductions, etc.

- Product: Develop methods for
monitoring product/service performance.
Ask what is working, what is not working
and what needs to change to work more
effectively. Consider re-packaging lower-
performing products with better
performing products to move inventory.

- Pricing: Develop methods for monitoring
and responding to pricing issues.
Determine how pricing affects sales of
your products. Can you increase your
pricing and not impact sales? If you
decrease pricing to increase sales, can you
still make sufficient revenue to be
profitable? Learn which products will
generate the highest margins.

- Placement: Develop methods to insure
that your products are available where
your customers are located. Be aware of

new markets that expand or enhance your target market share.

- Promotion: Monitor the media and initiate methods for determining which media tools are most effective for promoting each product or service. Note that some products may be more applicable to one market than another, and therefore, the best media to promote that product or service might be different.

- Strategic Partners: Develop methods for identifying Strategic Partners who could be instrumental in the positioning of your products and services to your target market and with new markets as well.

- **Finance Department Operations Plan**
  - The Finance Department's Mission is to:
    - Insure methods are in place to assure the highest Customer Satisfaction
    - Develop accounting processes
    - Develop and implement financial planning methods
    - Provide department organizational management and leadership
    - Communicate regularly with Management and other departments
    - Monitor, measure and report on KPI's
    - Support Corporate Mission

146

- Functions: There are Functions that are common to each Department such as: Processes, Personnel, Training, Budgets, Technology, Deliverables (KPI's), and Management Reports. Each Department Manager should coordinate its functions with management and other department operations.

- Tasks:
    - Customers: Finance people are frequently "black and white" thinkers. As a result, they may not interact well with customers. You owe us, or you don't. They may think the client owes and has no interest in discussing the matter. However, as the Owner, you need to insure that methods are in place so your staff interacts civilly with customers, even if they do owe you money. This is not to say you ignore or write-off monies that are owed to your company. If they owe you, they owe you. But handle the situation professionally. It's better to get "some than none!"

    - Investment: The finance department must establish a method for monitoring all investments (this includes loans, lines of credit, real estate investments, etc.). Pay back loans and other financial commitments as promised. These investors have put their trust, and their money, in your ability to launch and grow a successful business. They deserve frequent updates. Establish a method for communicating frequently with your financial partners. They need to feel they are a part of your team. And, you will find things go much smoother if you should have a problem down the road when you have maintained a strong communication link with them.

- Accounting System: Set-up your accounting system using approved methods for accounts receivable, accounts payable, for credit policies and collections. Bring in a specialist to set-up, and perhaps even handle your bookkeeping. Some ask me the difference between a bookkeeper and a CPA. The answer is involved, but a simple response I provide for my clients is that bookkeepers take care of your day to day finances, such as handling your checkbook, preparing and mailing invoices and collections. CPA's are more frequently used for tax purposes. The bookkeeper handles the accounting on a regular basis, and

148

then turns the financials over to the CPA to prepare and submit your taxes. For a more involved and complete answer, consult with a bookkeeper and a CPA.

- Taxes: File your taxes on time. Period. The IRS does not take lightly your failure to pay your taxes on time and in full. Get help if you need it. As the saying goes, "You can pay now or pay later, but you will pay." Set-side taxes for the day you will file your taxes. And, don't spend the money that has been allocated for taxes. IT IS NOT YOUR MONEY, SO DON'T THINK OF IT AS IF IT WERE.

- This is especially true in the area of payroll taxes. If you withhold taxes from your employees paycheck and fail to pay those taxes to the government you will be in serious trouble. Don't use other people's money.

- Financial Documents: Make sure you are in compliance with all financial documents, such as sales tax permits and other mandatory's required by local, state or federal agencies. Consult with a CPA to insure you are in compliance.

- Other: The finance department is at the heart of your business. If you don't understand finance and accounting, find someone who will help you - either internally, on an outsourced basis or even as a mentor who has your best interests at heart. There are too many stories of the entrepreneur who hired an employee who embezzled funds or just did not do their job the way they should have and suddenly the entrepreneur was faced with situations he never expected. Think of my earlier story of when I did not have anyone on-staff, or even outsourced, who I felt I could trust. I tried to do it all myself and ended up having meetings with the IRS. I didn't get an attorney or CPA/bookkeeper to help until I was trying to get OUT of business. Do not wait until you have problems to get help. Start out the right way.

- **The Legal Department**
  - The Legal Department's Mission is to
    - Insure methods are in place to assure the highest Customer Satisfaction

- Provide oversight of all legal matters which can affect the company
- Provide department organizational management and leadership
- Communicate regularly with Management and other departments
- Monitor, measure, and report on KPI's
- Support Corporate Mission

- Functions: There are Functions that are common to each Department such as: Processes, Personnel, Training, Budgets, Technology, Deliverables (KPI's), and Management Reports. Each Department Manager should coordinate its functions with management and other department operations.

- Tasks:
  - Structure: The Legal Department, whether an internal department or, which is more often the case, an outsourced service, needs to make the arrangements for the legal structure for the business. The company can become any one of a number of structures, depending on a number of factors. Again, this is where the Owner must call on competent counsel who will work on his behalf to organize the company properly.

- It is simple to set-up a sole proprietorship, but you, personally, are liable for the business. If someone sues the business, they have access to your personal assets. To insure your personal assets are protected you should consider a "Limited Liability Company" (LLC), a "Limited Liability Partnership" (LLP), a "Sub-S Corporation", or a "C-Corporation". Consult with your attorney and CPA to insure that you select the structure that is right for you and your investors/partners.

- I also encourage the completion of a formal partnership agreement between business owners, even husbands and wives, best friends and siblings. When you start the business you cannot imagine any way that you would ever have a misunderstanding. But, things do happen. Misunderstandings do occur. It's best to establish, upfront, the terms of the agreement and the method that will be utilized to dissolve the partnership.

- Contracts: During the life of a business, there will be numerous contracts and agreements. Lease agreements, employee policies, purchase agreements, etc. Most of us do not review contracts on a regular basis, so it is advisable to have a specialist available to look after your interests. But, again, you must remember that you, as the Owner, are responsible for the legal issues the business faces.

- Intellectual property: Protect your inventions, techniques and those items which make your business unique. There are attorneys who specialize in what is called "Intellectual Property".

- Litigation: Although you don't anticipate litigation for your business, it very likely will occur. Do not try to deal with it on your own. That's what attorneys do. Yes their fees may seem steep, but if they prove you were not at fault in a multi-million dollar suit, their fees are worthwhile. Have competent representation.

- Compliance: Legal counsel comes in all specialties. If you cannot afford a specialist in each area, or to hire a firm which has all the specialties on their staff, hire a good general counsel who has solid small business experience.

- **The Human Resource Department**

- The Human Resource Department's Mission is to:
    - Insure methods are in place to assure the highest Customer Satisfaction
    - Provide oversight of all HR matters that can affect the company
    - Provide department organizational management and leadership
    - Communicate regularly with Management and other departments
    - Monitor, measure, and report on KPI's
    - Support Corporate Mission

- Functions: There are Functions that are common to each Department such as: Processes, Personnel, Training, Budgets, Technology, Deliverables (KPI's), and Management Reports. Each Department Manager should coordinate its functions with management and other department operations.

- Tasks:
    - Benefits: Meet with a number of companies to identify the best types and sources for employee benefits. There are benefit companies that will provide quotes for your employees. The government has initiated some new health insurance legislation that will require the owner to look carefully at the type and extent to which they will cover employees in regards to health, disability and time off.

- Facilities: Some companies give the responsibility for the facilities to the Human Resource Manager. Whether or not this is the case in your company someone needs to be responsible for this area. It will cover leases, equipment (air conditioners, heaters, etc.) parking areas and repairs to the property.

- Health, Safety and Environmental (HSE): Many companies fail to understand the responsibility they have for the safety of their employees. In some industries this is so important there are people who specialize in this area. Be sure you have taken every step necessary, and then some, to insure that your employees are safe and that they know how important it is to provide a safe environment for your customers. This also includes appropriate training in health, safety and environmental issues.

- Insurance: Be sure that you have obtained the appropriate and adequate commercial insurance for your particular type of business.

- Training: The Human Resource Manager is typically responsible for researching and providing training for employees. They work with other departments to address specific training needs and develop and present general training to all employees. This is a critical step when hiring a new employee. They must be trained in all the important facets of their job and understand the expectations the company has for working with them.

- Recruiting: There are very specific requirements for how to identify, recruit, hire, train and fire employees. Make an appointment with your local state agency to learn the mandatory information in this area.

- Employee Policy Manual: Write one. Period. Then, be sure that every new-hire receives a copy and signs an agreement that they have read and agree to the terms stated in the Policy Manual.

- **The Sales Department**
  - The Sales Department's Mission is to:
    - Insure methods are in place to assure the highest Customer Satisfaction
    - Sell
    - Provide oversight of all Sales matters that can affect the company
    - Provide department organizational management and leadership

- Communicate regularly with Management and other departments
- Monitor, measure, and report on KPI's
- Support Corporate Mission

- Functions: There are Functions that are common to each Department such as: Processes, Personnel, Training, Budgets, Technology, Deliverables (KPI's), and Management Reports. Each Department Manager should coordinate its functions with management and other department operations.

- Tasks:
  - Sales Manual/Training: Although most sales people frown on procedure, it is critical to prepare a written sales manual that clearly explains the sales function, the processes, how territories are defined and, especially the compensation structure. If you address these four areas you will have covered about 90% of the problems you will experience working with the sales staff.

  - Sales Funnel: The sales funnel is a graphic representation of the sales process. The graphic shows eleven steps in the process. Your company may have less, but it probably will not have more. Sit down with the sales manager and discuss each step considering how you will be interacting with the customer and others within the company to accomplish that step. If the step, as presented here, is unnecessary, remove it from the funnel. The idea is for a sales manager to be able to know exactly where any sales prospect is in the sales funnel - are you still Qualifying (Stage 3) or has the relationship with the client progressed on to the negotiation stage (Stage 7).

In addition to knowing where each sales prospect is in the process, it also enables you to know when the sale will close (Stage 8) and how much revenue is expected from the close. If a salesperson has many sales prospects, but the value of each sale is low, perhaps they should be handling fewer prospects with a higher Return on Investment (ROI). This is an integral part of management's job. Sales people are happy as long as they are out selling. However, if they are not closing, or not closing enough of the right accounts, they are not helping the cash flow for the company as a whole. Being busy doesn't guarantee cash flow.

Sales Funnel

Sales Prospects

1. Unqualified prospects
2. Initial Communication
3. First Discussion
4. Develop Solution
5. Present Solution
6. Customer Evaluation
7. Negotiation
8. Obtain Verbal Commitment
9. Obtain Written Order
10. Deliver Order
11. Obtain Payment

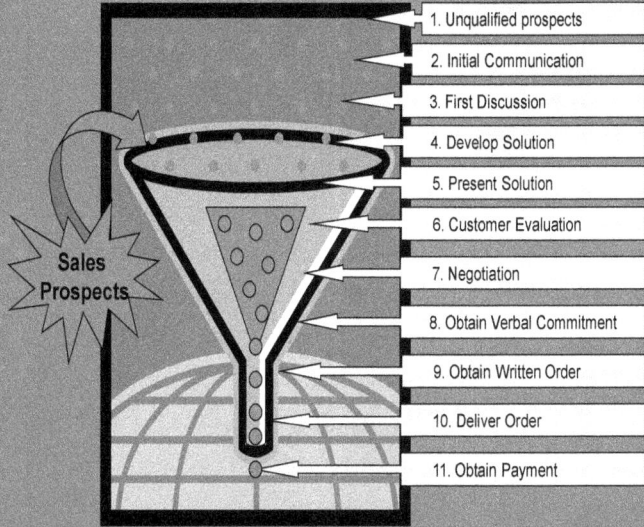

- Sales presentation: Prepare a standard sales presentation that covers all the key components of the Features, Advantages and Benefits (FAB's) of the products and services. Make sure to train all the sales people so they know the key "pitch points" for your products and services. Each will have their own style and delivery, but they need to cover the same material.

- **Customer Service Department**
  - The Customer Service Department's Mission is to:
    - Insure methods are in place to assure the highest Customer Satisfaction
    - Insure methods are in place (and encouraged) for frequent and open customer communication
    - Provide oversight of all Customer Service matters that can affect the company
    - Provide department organizational management and leadership
    - Communicate regularly with Management and other departments
    - Monitor, measure, and report on KPI's
    - Support Corporate Mission

  - Functions: There are Functions that are common to each Department such as: Processes, Personnel, Training, Budgets, Technology, Deliverables (KPI's), and Management Reports. Each Department Manager should coordinate its functions with management and other department operations.

  - Tasks:
    - Customer Service Policy: Customers are the life blood of any business. As the Owner you have the responsibility to establish the policy for working with your customers. Emphasize the policy

repeatedly - to your customers, your suppliers and your other stakeholders.

- Some companies seem to fear that their customers will take advantage of them. It's hard to do that when a company has clearly defined and visible policies about how they will deal with customers. Give your employees the latitude to work as they feel appropriate (within certain guidelines) when addressing a customer's concern. And let them know you will stand behind their decisions.

- The hotel business is a good example of how the "Customer is King". You will long remember the hotel that responds negatively (or not at all) to a concern you have, while you will be eager to tell others of the great service they provided when you faced an issue. Yes there will be those who will try to take advantage of the system. But the ones who appreciate good customer service will far out-weigh the naysayers.

- Touch Points: As the Owner, step back from your business and identify all the places where your business "touches" someone else - all your stakeholders.

For instance, the receptionist who answers the phone is typically one of the first "Touch Points" a customer, supplier, investor, or potential employee will have of your company. Make sure the experience is a positive one. This applies to everyone who can impact the client's views of your company-even the guy who packs and ships the client's order on the loading dock is responsible for a touch point. If the customer opens the box and the product was packed properly, they have a good experience. If the product was NOT packed properly, you have a negative touch point.

- Feedback: Establish methods for monitoring customer attitudes. This can range from customer survey cards to the website where you are encouraged to go to "complete a survey about your dining experience". Then, offer an incentive for taking the survey which will drive them back to the restaurant or establishment. Do not forget that when a customer completes one of these surveys you have their email address. As the Owner, send them a personal email thanking them for coming to your establishment Ask if they mind periodic emails asking about their shopping experience and encourage them to stay in touch with you regarding future visits. Essentially, they have just been added to your informal "Advisory Board".

- Results from these surveys and customer responses should be shared with all employees (you do not want to share the customer's name). Share the good, the bad and the ugly. That way your employees know that you are being upfront with them about the customer experience and will understand when you make changes in the operations of the business to accommodate the customer issues.

- **Operation/Production Department**
  - The Operation/Production Department's Mission is to:
    - Insure methods are in place to assure the highest Customer Satisfaction
    - Provide oversight of all operations/production matters that can affect the company (manufacturing, safety, quality control)
    - Provide department organizational management and leadership

- Communicate regularly with Management and other departments
- Monitor, measure, and report on KPI's
- Support Corporate Mission

- Functions: There are Functions that are common to each Department such as: Processes, Personnel, Training, Budgets, Technology, Deliverables (KPI's), and Management Reports. Each Department Manager should coordinate its functions with management and other department operations.

- Tasks:
  - Production Standards Manual: Put it in writing! You, as the Owner, along with your Production/Operations Department Manager are responsible for establishing the standards by which your operations staff will work. Insure that all production personnel are fully aware of the production standards and expectations - especially with regards to safety and health requirements. (Those signs that encourage employees to wash their hands before returning to work are not just for show!)

    - For instance, if you run a sandwich shop and customers are walking in front of the counter indicating the items they want on their sandwich, the "sandwich builder" should make sure the area is kept clean. Little things like this add to the positive purchase experience. It is, as we've said earlier, another "Touch Point".

- Production schedules: Insure that the staff know and adhere to the production schedules. If a product is scheduled for delivery by Tuesday at 2PM, they have a responsibility to deliver by Tuesday at 2PM. No questions. No excuses. That's it. Failure to meet a due date is unacceptable. Do not promise to deliver if you cannot deliver when promised. Factor in the time required by outside suppliers and vendors. Emphasize that your business depends on their meeting the schedules. Additionally, their business depends on you getting the order - now and in the future.

- Quality Control: Quality is in the eye of the beholder (translated: Customer). Your idea of "quality" or "good enough" must meet the customer's expectations, or you will not be in business very long. Insure your Operations/Production Manager understands the expectations and shares those expectations with the staff.

- Distribution/Delivery: Insure that the Distribution and Delivery system is working well. Periodically spend time with the distributors and insure that you are aware of the issues they face which may be detrimental to your business success

- **The Information Technology (IT) Department**
  - The Information Technology (IT) Department's Mission is to:
    - Insure methods are in place to assure the highest Customer Satisfaction
    - Provide oversight of all IT matters that can affect the company (Operating system, Hardware, Software, Installation, Maintenance)
    - Provide department organizational management and leadership
    - Communicate regularly with Management and other departments
    - Monitor, measure, and report on KPI's
    - Support Corporate Mission

  - Functions: There are Functions that are common to each Department such as: Processes, Personnel, Training, Budgets, Technology, Deliverables (KPI's), and Management Reports. Each Department Manager should coordinate its functions with management and other department operations.
  - Tasks:
    - Identify/select operating system: The Technology Department must work with each of the other departments of the

company as well as your customers. They play a vital role in insuring that the company communication systems are functioning as efficiently as possible. They must be willing to work the extra hours to "keep the system up and running", so you do not lose orders or fail to deliver on the orders you do get.

- Select Hardware: Working with the other department managers, the IT Department should review the environment and make hardware recommendations that will enable each department to function at peak capacity, but also within a budget and as efficiently as possible. Remember that the IT Department is responsible for computer and telecommunication equipment.

- Select Software: Likewise, the IT Department should work closely with each department to insure that the proper software is acquired and the appropriate individuals are trained so that the investment pays off.

- Installation: IT Staff will be responsible for installing all the hardware and software. Yes, the team may use outside vendors for some applications, but, ultimately, the IT Manager/Staff are responsible for the day-to-day operations.

- Maintenance: As stated earlier the Owner/Entrepreneur should work closely to insure that the IT Department maintains all the equipment so there is no "down time." Down time, during office hours (and with today's cyber world office hours are actually 24/7/365) is a killer for a business, especially a small business.

Soft Launch

Each department will have specific duties to accomplish prior to the official launch. Each department must test its processes, personnel and practices to insure you are really ready for business.

Launch: Now, "Launch" your business and all the processes and KPI's to monitor your progress.

The Bottom Line...

Remember that ultimately, the company's Mission and Milestones should support your own personal Mission!

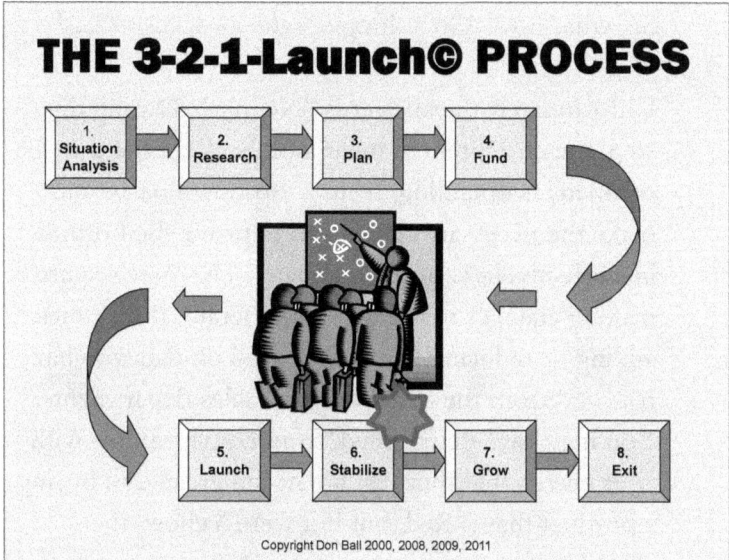

THE 3-2-1-Launch© PROCESS

Copyright Don Ball 2000, 2008, 2009, 2011

So, you have launched your business. You have developed job descriptions, processes and KPI's to monitor performance. You have your marketing department sending out high-quality marketing materials promoting your brand to your target market. Your sales team meets with a pre-agreed number of prospects each week and you get a report each Monday morning comparing projected sales against the finance department's report on revenue and expenses. Legal issues are being dealt with on a professional and expedited basis using competent attorneys. Your systems of hiring and providing technology for your employees and customers are working well. And, operations are functioning smoothly, based on customer surveys and personal calls you, as the Owner are making.

So, what now? Go golfing or take a vacation?

Unfortunately the answer is "Neither". During this step, the entrepreneur must look back on the way the company is operating, from a top-down basis, and make the necessary changes to improve the bottom-line effectiveness of the company. This may require making changes in the way you operate. It may mean adding or reducing your staff based on data you have received from the marketing and sales departments. You may have determined, from conversations with your clients that they just are not interested in buying a product that is Red, but if it were Yellow, they would buy every one you can make.

As the Owner you would never know this information if you are busy making sandwiches, cutting the grass or changing the oil. Yes, you will probably still be doing that to a degree, but when the company expects you to do everything, you are no longer in the driver's seat of your stage coach; you are back to riding the horses. To make management decisions and insure the company is moving forward with the right vision and direction, you must stay in the seat of your stage coach!

This stage involves the steps to stabilize the day-to-day operations of the venture by developing a solid foundation for the business. The Owner will need to call on department managers, bankers, financial, HR, legal advisors, realtors and marketing specialists for assistance and guidance. It is more important, however, for the Owner to develop a relationship with the company's clients.

Many Owners never seem to understand the value their Customers bring to the business beyond the purchases they make. A smart business owner will form a "Customer Advisory Board" (formal or not) to whom the owner can turn, to insure that the company is meeting the demands, expectations and needs of its customers. I tell my clients that to be a successful Owner you must take off your "Owner Hat" and put on your "Customer Hat" to make decisions for the business with the customer at the forefront of the decision process. Customers will tell you what they want if you will just ask. In fact they wish you would!

There are three basic steps in this stage:
- Begin manufacturing, production and delivery of the finished product.
- Implement methods and procedures for monitoring performance (Department and Company)
- Make adjustments where required

It's time to start doing what you wanted this business to do. You have launched your business and you are getting clients, so now you are filling orders. Watch this step closely, especially in the early days. If you have not established the processes for manufacturing and producing your products you will be scrambling around "hoping" things go right.

But as the smart Owner that you are, I am sure that you have established solid processes and policies and now you can focus on producing a quality product.

You will accomplish this by implementing methods and procedures for monitoring the performance of the Company and the individual departments. Since you established Processes for running the business, Reports which will be submitted to you on a regular basis (and which, if appropriate, you will submit to your stakeholders) and you have identified the methods for communicating and managing your people, your job as the owner will be much more organized and successful. Monitor each KPI carefully, not just to monitor the performance, but also to check that you are monitoring the right performance metrics.

Are you measuring and monitoring the right things? Are there problems you did not expect that you need to watch more closely?

Make the adjustments to your processes, reports and people as necessary to insure your business is operating as effectively and as efficiently as possible. Especially in the first year the Owner should review the company's performance with their mentors/advisory team and stakeholders on a regular basis; communicate regularly with employees (remember that they came on-board with your start-up business with faith in your ability to guide this new venture to success); and make the changes (even if they may be difficult financially, with the staff and with suppliers) necessary to fine tune your operation.

Some Owners join "CEO Roundtables" to share problems and solutions with others who may be facing a similar situation. Obviously, it is more important to have a coach or mentor to call on for advice.

Your stakeholders will certainly appreciate this approach!

The Bottom Line…

You, as the Owner, must see the big picture for the business, identify changes necessary to be more effective, make the changes and move forward to the next goal.

Stage 7: Grow

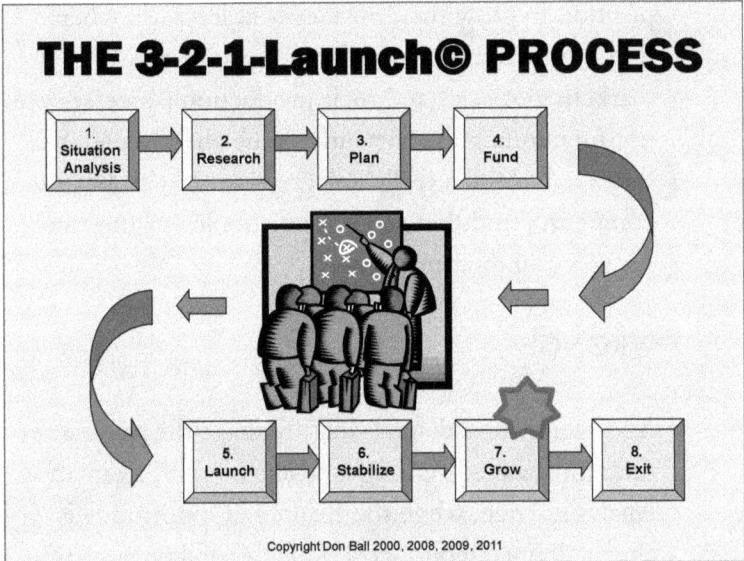

THE 3-2-1-Launch© PROCESS

| 1. Situation Analysis | 2. Research | 3. Plan | 4. Fund |
| 5. Launch | 6. Stabilize | 7. Grow | 8. Exit |

Copyright Don Ball 2000, 2008, 2009, 2011

Michael Gerber, author of "e-Myth Revisited"[7], advises entrepreneurs to organize their businesses as a "franchise prototype". Even if a person has no desire to open additional locations, the point is to build a business that you are working "ON", not working "IN". You need an operation that you can duplicate.

The GROWTH Stage may be years beyond your launch date. But if you do not plan for it FROM the launch date, you will never really be able to position yourself for the growth you want in the way you want it.

---

[7] "e-Myth Revisited" by Michael Gerber

In fact, I have many clients who come to me asking that I assist them with "growing" their business. Discussions usually reveal that they are not in a position to grow their business - at least not when they come to me. They still have problems with marketing or sales and their production processes are not functioning as efficiently as they had hoped. But they "...have this really great opportunity to buy out a competitor and that acquisition should..." they feel, "...solve all their problems..."

WRONG!

An Owner should approach this stage the same way they approached starting a business - with a Situation Analysis. Then, when the Business Opportunity is clearly defined, conduct serious Feasibility Research, followed by a written Business Plan (merging your current operation with the new business idea). Often, this stage is followed by a search for Funding and a "Re-Launch" of the new business.
Does this process sound familiar?

Yes, the key to growing your business is to go back to "square one", Situation Analysis and proceed through each step to the launch of your NEW business idea. Although it may sound easy, you know now that it is not. Growing a business requires the same depth of personal evaluation, research and planning as you originally applied to start your venture. Perhaps more, because now you have even more "stakeholders" than when you started. Now you have all those employees and their families…

An Owner may approach this Stage a number of times in the lifecycle of the business. But, approaching the growth of your business without a plan makes the task daunting to say the least.

The Objective is to identify, evaluate, select and launch a growth model that is right for your business…each time. As we have discussed in earlier chapters, you will need the support and guidance of your department managers, bankers, financial, HR, legal advisors, realtors and marketing specialists to chart a plan for growing the business. Again, and equally important, is the input from your clients. If you have a relationship with your clients, they will tell you whether your ideas for growth are on-target or not.

Stage 1-A: Situation Analysis

In this step, go back and review your current situation. You have been in business for a while, so you will have much more data to pull from. Consider:

- Personal Situation: When you first considered starting your own business you asked yourself a number of critical, personal questions. Given the position you are in now, as a business owner considering growth of your business, ask yourself the same questions:

What is your <u>motivation</u> for being a business owner? Has it changed since you became a business owner?

Evaluate your life in terms of <u>Employment</u>. You are the "Boss" now, not an "employee". How do you feel about that? Has your attitude toward the work environment changed since you started this venture? Would you rather go back to being an employee? If so, that is fine. If you like being the "Boss", that is okay, too. But now you are looking at both options through the eyes of one with experience. When you started your business you had no idea what to expect. Now, you do. Act on what you know to be the truth.

What about your <u>Education and Expertise?</u> When you first considered becoming an entrepreneur you had to build your business on the education and experience you had at that point. What have you learned since you started your business that you never expected – both the good and the bad?

Perhaps you thought it would be easy to sell your product…but it has not been so easy. You thought it would be easy to "tell others what to do", and they would do it. But they do not. You thought your family members were giving you the money to start your business and would support you "regardless of what happens to their investment"…but they have become a bit cooler to you through the years. You thought everyone would pay you what they owed you, when they owed it to you, in full. But, they do not. Perhaps you have learned that it's a real rush to see the excitement on the face of your customers when they buy or use your products. Maybe you have finally come to an understanding that those math problems in high school and college were representative of "real life"!

Sound familiar? You will probably agree that you have learned a lot since you launched your business. Take all that you have learned and factor it into the plans you have for moving forward. What would you do differently in this next stage of your business?

How has your <u>Financial Situation</u> changed since you opened the business? Be honest. Are you paying yourself yet? Are you personally deeper in debt? How is your credit score? You know the impact your personal finances can have on getting credit. Perhaps you should stabilize your credit situation before adding to it (assuming lenders would give you more money).

How is your <u>Physical Situation</u>? On a scale of 1 to 10, with 10 being the best, how is your health? More specifically, how is your blood pressure? How about your cholesterol? Have you contracted any diseases or conditions that could impact your ability to grow your business? Look seriously at how the business has impacted your health. Are you suffering from conditions due to long hours and high stress? How is the "ticker"? Do you really think that adding to your company will decrease your stress levels?

As if health was not enough, perhaps one of the most important of the personal areas an entrepreneur should consider is each of the Stakeholders who are looking to you with some expectations. You still have your family, who are the most important stakeholders. They have certain, very justifiable, expectations of you. And, then there are the others; like suppliers, customers, lenders and of course, all the employees who look to you for the support of their stakeholders…their families and loved ones. So, it is probably no surprise that your blood pressure is high and now you have developed an ulcer! Ask yourself how growing your business will enable you to do a better job of meeting the realistic expectations of your stakeholders. If it will, then push on, valiant entrepreneur!

I would say that by the time you have arrived at the point of considering how to grow your business, you have gained an extensive amount of Business Management Experience. You might recall when I shared at the beginning of this book that I started my business understanding how to do marketing and trade shows, but knew nothing about running a business. My business failed before I could catch on to the steps I needed to initiate before it went under. Since then, I have read and studied and asked mentors questions so that I could learn what a person really needs to know to survive in the jungle of business ownership. As they say, "…*if I had a dime for each lesson I've learned…*" What have you learned in the area of managing a business that will help you to GROW a business?

I have another question. Have you ever grown a business? If not, you might want to bring in someone who has, to help you - just like you developed your advisory board to help you launch your business initially.

- Business Opportunities/Threats: The bottom line is to honestly evaluate the business opportunities and treats your business faces at this point.
  - Business Opportunities: List the business opportunities you are considering. Write down what it would mean to your current personal and business situation if you pursued each one.
  - Business Threats: Along with the opportunities, list the threats that your business faces if you do not grow. Would you lose key employees? Are your competitors adding new products that may make your product offering obsolete?

- Situation Analysis Summary: Summarize what you have learned about yourself personally and from a business perspective.

  - Goals: Evaluate your progress with the business thus far in terms of the goals you established before you started. Have you reached some, most or all of your goals? Why or why not? Are the goals still important to you and your stakeholders? Now, establish new goals for yourself and your business, along with due dates and the action steps to accomplish the goals.

- Metrics for Success: Look back at the metrics you selected when you first started your business. Do those same metrics apply? Are there other metrics that are more feasible and reasonable? Identify, and record, the metrics for continuing your success.

- Barriers to Success: You identified the Barriers to Success when you first considered starting a business. How have those barriers impacted your success or failure? Identify the NEW Barriers to Success for growing the business.

- Options: Just as before, list the options you are considering. Perhaps you are considering adding a new product line, opening a new location or adding a new department. You might be considering the acquisition of a product or company or "Going International". List each one with a brief description.

- Summarize the "Concept": Now, rank those options in terms of what you want to do and what, at least without the benefit of more extensive research, will enable you to accomplish your personal and business goals. The one at the top of your list is the "Concept" which you will research to determine the feasibility and how it will impact your current business and your personal life.

Stage 2-A: Feasibility Research

- **Motivation:** When you were originally planning to have a business you started by indicating the Motivation customers would have to use your products and services. You now have actual clients you can ask to determine their interest in your products and services. This is perhaps the most valuable asset you have as a business owner. Customers.

  And, if you have developed a relationship with them, they can provide you with more exact information about their buying habits and patterns.

- **Market**
  - Market segments: Look at your current market segments and then indicate the additional market segments you will pursue. If your "Concept" centers around the same market segment you are currently targeting be sure you have the latest data on that group.

  - Buyers: Identify and define as specifically as possible those who will ultimately authorize the purchase of your product or service. It may be "mom" who is buying groceries, or the Purchasing Manager at a Fortune 500 Company. The more you know about the buyer the more apt you are to launch a successful growth strategy.

- Influencers: Influencers are those who can influence the buyers to place an order. Identify the individuals who have the ear of your buyers. You might recall we used the example of the child who wants to buy a candy bar when Mom is checking out at the grocery store. The child is the influencer on Mom who is the buyer.

- Strategic Partners: Is there anyone you can partner with to reach either the influencer or the buyer? Find another company that you can support and who can get you in front of your target market. For instance, a printer client introduced a new product, a mud flap that companies could use to place their advertising message. I got them together with another client who did not have trucks, but ran a large distribution warehouse and knew a lot of transportation companies. The warehouse client needed printing and the printer needed access to trucking companies. It was a good match for both.

- Organizations: Evaluate the support that trade organizations/associations and Chambers of Commerce can provide with lists of local companies as well as local area demographics.

- Competitors: Will your growth pit your company against new competitors or will you be facing the same ones, but with new products and services? Evaluate the competitive landscape to see how your company's growth will impact your competitive position in the marketplace.

- **Magic:** Describe your new products and services as succinctly as possible. Include data to support your competitive position and include data regarding manufacturing/production costs, as well as Features, Advantages and Benefits (FAB's).

- **Model:** Will the growth of your business require you to consider a new or modified model for your business? If you are changing the model be sure to consider the impact of that on your current operations. How will your employees and customers be affected by the change?

- **Mandatories:** As a business owner you are probably familiar with the permits and licenses that were required for you to be operational. However, you should insure that you meet the mandatory's necessary for your growth plans.

- **Media:** You know the importance of a strong media program to promote your businesses' products and services by now. However, consider media now in terms of your growth strategy. Will this growth require an expanded media effort? Will you need different types of media than you have used before? Can you leverage your current media buy to get a better rate by adding more advertising for the new program? Consult with your marketing management to identify the best way for you to market the new business.

- **Management:** The market is important, as are the products and services, but the people issues are even more critical when you are growing your business. You will need to have all your team on-board with your decision to grow your business whether it is acquiring another company, launching a new product or opening a new location.

  - Mentors: It is important to have mentors when you start and run your business, but it is equally important to have skilled professionals help when you consider growing your business. Just like when you started your business, you are entering new territory. Find others with growth experience to help you plan and launch the next stage of your business.

  - Key Managers: Growing your business takes market research, and with an existing team of managers and a support staff, it requires a concentrated focus on the impact to that team. How will you utilize their capabilities in the new venture? If you are acquiring another company, how will the mix of the two cultures impact your management team?

- **Method (Strategies)**
  - Marketing Strategy: How will you adjust your Marketing Strategy to launch the new venture?

- Personnel Strategy: How will your Personnel Strategy change with the new venture?

- Production/Operations Strategy: How will the growth plans you are considering impact the current and future production and operations for the company?

- Financial Strategy: You may have all your proverbial "ducks in a row" for your business now. How will this new venture affect your financial situation? How do you plan to remain a strong company, financially, and grow at the same time? (This is a good time to have a solid financial expert on your team!)

- Customer Strategy: Perhaps one of the most critical components is to insure that you do not lose market share, but in fact grow market share. Without the support of your customers you are dead in the water!

- Management Strategy: Prepare a written statement that describes the way you will utilize your current management team and how you plan to grow your company with forward-thinking managers.

- **Money:** Running a business is all about the numbers. As a successful business owner you know that now. It's taken attention to every detail, especially financially, to bring the company to the point where you are considering a growth strategy. The same basic components apply now that you considered when you first started your business:

- Revenue Streams: Your growth plan must include a description of the new revenue streams for the business. If you are opening a new location, you will have additional revenue coming from a new geographical location. If you are launching a new product it should, obviously, represent a new revenue stream.

  - Expenses: Conversely, growth isn't all about additional revenue. With a new location there is also the expense of build-out and new employees. You will also need to consider marketing and supply support. There may be some economies of scale, but calculate them carefully. Bring in each of your eight departments to research the impact the growth plans will have on their specific area.

  - Funding: By now you have learned a great deal about funding your business. Credits, and a solid banking relationship, are even more critical when you are considering the funding for your growth. This is the time you will be glad you developed and maintained a strong relationship with your banker.

  - Financial Summary: Summarize the financial situation (Revenue streams, Expenses and

Funding) in a single paragraph. Does the
paragraph paint a solid financial picture that
will support growing your venture?

- **Measurement/Milestones:** Establish the milestones
for growing the business and how you will measure
your progress. It is a good idea to also include the
name of those responsible for each step and any
budgetary considerations.

Stage 3-A: Plan

- **Personal Strategic Plan:** Review your "old"
Personal Strategic Plan (the one you developed when
you first launched your business.) How are you doing
against your plan? Now, ask yourself how your
planned growth will help you accomplish those
personal goals. If it won't, you might want to
reconsider how you will grow the business.

- **Business Plan:** Using the same format as your first
Business Plan, prepare a new plan including the
findings of your research. In this Business Plan,
however, you will include historical data based on the
time you have been in business. You will want to
highlight any accomplishments the company has
made, the longevity and performance of key
employees and, especially, report on your financial
picture since the beginning of the business (or at least
the previous three years).

Stage 4A: Fund

- **Know how much you will need:** Your updated Business Plan will reveal how much additional funding you will need to expand and grow your business. Be realistic, though. You have probably learned some valuable lessons about under-capitalizing a business, or obtaining more funds than you needed (which is rare!). You also have experience writing a check to pay your loan note each month. You are about to increase that payment. Are you confident in your ability to generate sufficient revenue to cover the note and still remain profitable?

- **Know the source of the funds:** The same resources (loans, lines of credit, credit cards, venture capitalists, angel investors, and the tried and true…friends and family) that existed when you started your business are still there, although changes in the market place could have adversely affected the economy and credit may be tighter. Again, you will be especially thankful for having developed and maintained a solid banking relationship through the years.

- **Know the requirements for obtaining those funds:** Lenders may have new criteria (higher credit scores, perhaps) or they may only be willing to loan for additional capital that they can take as collateral. Maintain a strong relationship with your financing partners to determine what they can do, and on what terms. I recently had a client that had already built and was operating two successful hotels. He had invested about 15% of his own money in the first two deals

($5 Million and $4.2 Million respectively) He had plans to build a third hotel (valued at $12Million) which he was prepared to put up to 20% of his own money into. He informed me that the best deal he had been offered was for him to put up 45% cash and his two hotels as collateral. He decided to just wait until the economy turned around and, subsequently, put the entire project on hold.

Stage 5A: Launch

- **Pre-Launch:** Once you have obtained the financing for your growth or expansion, sit down with all your managers and go through the steps to modify your business operations to incorporate the expansion. Begin by reviewing and editing the overall Corporate Strategic Operations Plan. Share the revisions and new focus with your current management staff. Then they should be required to review and modify their own individual Department Strategic Operations Plans.

  Once the plans have been approved it will be time to implement the new strategies into the company's structure. Of critical importance is the review and development of new processes and KPI's for the company, plus the new criteria and content for the management reports the owner will submit to the financial stakeholders.

- **Soft Launch:** There will be a "settling in" period when the old operation will begin implementing the new operations. This is a critical stage for your company. I once worked with a company that acquired a company which manufactured products that were complimentary to our products and services. It was a good arrangement for both companies. However, a critical component was the merging of two personnel structures - one was union-based, the other was not. There were some sleepless nights as Human Resource Management worked through the issues to become one unified company with a single focus.

- **Launch:** Once the company structure has been revised and updated it is time to "officially" announce the new company to the world. Not surprisingly, it probably will not be a surprise to anyone. But, now it's "official".

Stage 6A: Stabilize

The same steps apply with the new organization which you applied when starting your first company:

- Begin manufacturing/production and delivery of finished product.

- Implement methods and procedures for monitoring performance (Department and Company)
- Make adjustments where required

Stage 7A: Grow (Again)

Now…go back and do it all over again!

- **Situation Analysis**
- **Feasibility Research**
- **Planning**
- **Funding**
- **Stabilize**
- **Grow…**

The Bottom Line…

The Bottom Line is to develop a plan for growing the company that will merge well with your current operation with a minimal amount of disruption. Be sure to bring in your advisory team for assistance.

Stage 8: Exit

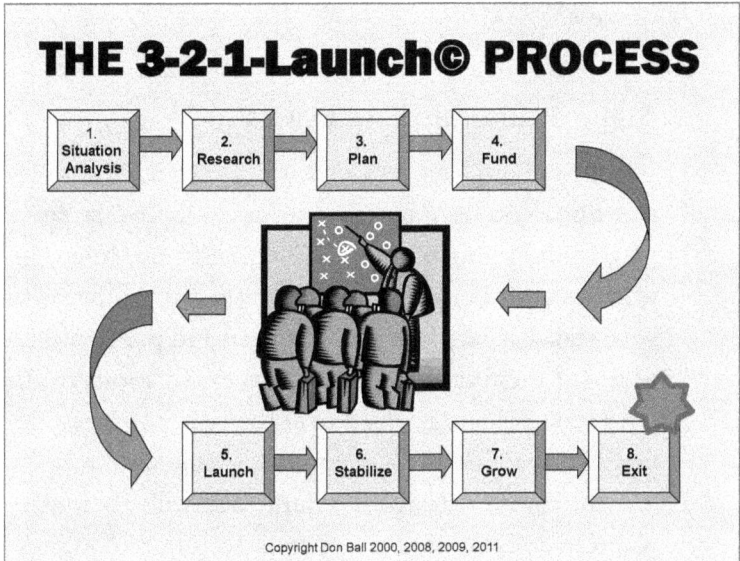

THE 3-2-1-Launch© PROCESS

1. Situation Analysis → 2. Research → 3. Plan → 4. Fund

5. Launch → 6. Stabilize → 7. Grow → 8. Exit

Copyright Don Ball 2000, 2008, 2009, 2011

This stage takes into consideration the steps to exit the business. There are a number of options: Drain all the money out of the business and close it, sell it, pass it on to family members, merge with another company that sees value to their company by acquiring the assets of your company, etc. Frankly, the best option is dependent upon a number of variables, best discussed with the owner's attorney, CPA and personal financial advisor and especially your family. It is also best to begin the actual EXIT process early-on in the life of the business. In fact, if possible some financial planners recommend including the exit strategy in the initial business plan.

The process for developing and launching an Exit Strategy is similar to that of a new entrepreneur. Go back to Stage I: Situation Analysis to begin the process.

Stage 1: Situation Analysis:

In this step, go back and review your current situation. You have been in business for a while, so you will have much more data to pull from. Re-evaluate your Personal Situation, especially in terms of your stakeholders and your financial and personal goals for the future. How have the expectations from your stakeholders evolved over the years? How do you anticipate them changing in the time until you actually exit the business? Your health will, obviously, play a major role in some of your decisions. You may want to accelerate your plans for exiting. Or, you may want to phase out your exit over a longer period of time, bringing in and training someone else to assume your role. You may want to totally separate yourself from the business (a challenge for someone who has worked to launch and grow a successful venture!).

Do you want to move to your own island, or do you want to do something else with your time like gardening or serving on other company boards? These are all serious questions which you should discuss with your advisors. Once you have evaluated your personal situation and your business ideas, decide on the option that is best for you and your family. This, as you know by now, is your "Concept".

Stage 2: Feasibility Research:

Working with your team of advisors (Financial Planner, Attorney, CPA, Doctor, and others from whom you value their counsel) do your research. Your idea may, or may not, be feasible. If you want to pursue your Concept, but it doesn't seem feasible now, identify the steps to make it feasible.

This is the point where you will be glad that you started this process earlier rather than later. For instance, your goal to sell the company to a competitor may not be feasible if there are divisions of the company that would make such an acquisition unattractive to another company. You may need time to position a division or department, or even a product line as attractive to a smaller competitor, so another company will come along and buy your bigger operation.

See why it's important to have a team of advisors working with you?

Stage 3: Plan:

Write out, as you have in the past, your Personal Strategic Plan. Actually, by now, you should be "editing" rather than writing a new plan. Based on your current and anticipated personal situation, identify those activities and objectives that you want to accomplish. Then, write down the steps your business will have to take to accomplish your personal goals. Again, it's important to have a team of professionals assist you with this step.

Stage 4: Fund:

If you have been working with a conscientious financial planner he/she should have helped you identify your personal financial needs long before you are ready to exit the business. If you do not have a financial planner, now is the time! Bring in professional assistance to guide you toward the personal financial objectives you have established for yourself and your family.

Just as when you were establishing and growing your business, you should consider the following, but on more of a personal basis.

- **Know how much you will need.** This is a difficult decision that your financial planner can, and should be able to assist with. They will sit down with you to look at your personal needs, your commitments, the expectations of you and those around you and develop a strategy to achieve those objectives.

- **Know the source of the funds.** If you sell the business, there may be cash involved. Or, there may be stock or some other form of income. Carefully consider the tax implications for each.

- **Know the requirements for obtaining those funds.** Identify the steps you must take with your business to insure that the funds are available when you leave the business.

Stage 5: Launch:

Prepare your game plan for the exit. A properly developed exit strategy may take years to accomplish. Look not only at your own exit, but the impact it will have on others (your stakeholders). If the business will stay in operation, who will assume the reins when you step down? What can/should you do to prepare that person to take over, and what should you do to insure the employees of the company will not be adversely affected? Each department will have an impact on the steps to assure your smooth exit from the business and the businesses' transition to a new leader. Determine the action steps necessary to insure that the plan is going according to plan.

Stage 6: Stabilize:

Just as when you monitored each growth stage, develop and monitor carefully the KPI's for each department. There may be factors which adversely impact the business and which can threaten or accelerate your exit from the business. Surround yourself with your team of advisors to insure all aspects of your exit strategy are being monitored and the right decisions are being made.

Stage 8: Exit:

Now is the time to "head for the hills", as we say in Texas. In fact, I have a business associate who is planning his exit and each weekend he travels to the Hill Country of Texas to work on the house he and his wife will move to once he is ready to exit the business. He has been planning and working toward his exit from the business for years.

Bottom Line...

You might recall that one goal of business ownership is to help you achieve your Personal Strategic Plan. This stage helps an entrepreneur to set in motion a series of steps to accomplish those goals.

- Evaluate your current and anticipated situation and develop a series of options
- Research the options and determine which ones are most feasible
- Prepare a written Personal Strategic Plan and draft a new Business Plan for the venture which allows for your exit from the business
- Fund the exit, both from a personal and a business perspective
- Launch the exit plan action step
- Monitor and adjust the plan as necessary to insure that the exit strategy will meet your personal objectives

The Spiritual Dimension

Where I am today is because of God's guidance, mercy, forgiveness and love.

Although some entrepreneurs consider themselves "self-made successes", in reality there is One much greater beside them. If you plan to start a business, how would you factor in your spiritual commitment and service? These are just as important when you are an entrepreneur as when you are working for someone else because you set the tone and ethical culture for your business by the way you work with your customers, your suppliers and your employees.

There are times in almost every entrepreneur's life when they feel weak and vulnerable to situations seemingly beyond their control and comprehension. Although they will call on mentors and friends for help, they should first call on the One who is much mightier and wiser than all the mentors for guidance and peace. In fact, Paul reminded Timothy that, *"7For God did not give us a spirit of timidity, but a spirit of power, of love and of self-discipline."* (2 Timothy 1:7)[8]

Granted this passage is a part of a letter to Timothy to encourage him to be strong in his faith and

---

[8] All Passages taken from the New International Version, www.BibleGateway.com

commitment to Christ. I believe, however, that it can be equally powerful when we apply it to our attitude as a business owner.

Our source of power (and wisdom, too, according to James 1: 5) is God. Too many entrepreneurs and small business owners believe they are all by themselves. That to "Be the Boss", they must know everything and have all the answers. While I would encourage entrepreneurs to keep learning every day, they should remember they have access to the most powerful being in the world: God.

If God wants your business to be successful, and you apply yourself as if you believe that it can, then it will be. Look at Moses and Paul and Abraham… And, remember what the Psalmist, David, said in Psalms 25: 15: *15 My eyes are ever on the LORD, for only he will release my feet from the snare."*

We must learn to trust God to be there with us and for us. Trust is an integral part of the relationship we should have with God, as well. In Proverbs 3:5 and 6 we are encouraged to, *"Trust in the LORD with all your heart and lean not on your own understanding; in all your ways acknowledge him, and he will make your paths straight."*

Wow! What a powerful message of confidence this passage paints for us as entrepreneurs! This reminds me of my suggestions to surround yourself with an advisory team who have your best interests at heart.

Look at your spiritual life seriously. You may feel that you are totally in charge of your destiny. But wouldn't it be wiser to call on the One who is in control of everything, and everyone, in the universe?

From a Spiritual perspective, consider:

Integrity

(Defined as: Adherence to a code of moral, artistic or other values) Integrity comes from within. It forms the basis for your decisions regarding the business - how you deal with employees, those to whom you owe money, those who owe you money, your customers, your employees and the community in which you work.

It has been said "To be of real service you must give something which cannot be bought or measured with money, and that is sincerity and integrity". A Russian proverbs states, "With lies you may go ahead in the world, but you can never go back."

The Psalmist, in a prayer recorded in Psalms 25: 21 reminds us *"May integrity and uprightness protect me, because my hope is in you."* Earlier in the same chapter (25:2), he stated, *"...in you I trust, O my God. Do not let me be put to shame, nor let my enemies triumph over me."* And his son, Solomon, proclaimed, *"1 Better a poor man whose walk is*

blameless than a fool whose lips are perverse."
(Proverbs 19:1).

But, Christ brought the message of integrity home when He told His disciples *"Whoever can be trusted with very little can also be trusted with much, and whoever is dishonest with very little will also be dishonest with much. ¹¹So if you have not been trustworthy in handling worldly wealth, who will trust you with true riches?"* (Luke 16:10-11).

This brings up another point... Did you notice that Christ does not define "true riches" as "worldly wealth"? True riches go beyond the money we accumulate. They come from the relationships we develop with friends, family, employees (and their families), customers, suppliers, lenders...yes, with all our stakeholders!

Trust

(Defined as: Assured reliance on the character, ability, strength, or truth of something or someone.) Your stakeholders (those who depend on you) trust you. This is a trait that is often ignored or downplayed in the business world, but building trust in, and of, those around you will go a long way toward establishing lasting relationships and contribute to the success of your business. We know that we are more inclined to trust those who exhibit trust in us. But, as one said, "Trust, but verify"!

The writer of Proverbs explains the importance of trust in Proverbs 3: 3- 4, *"Let love and faithfulness never leave you; bind them around your neck, write them on the tablet of your heart. Then you will win favor and a good name in the sight of God and man."*

Sacrifice

(Defined as: Something given up or lost; to suffer loss of, renounce, injure or destroy for an ideal, belief or end) As an entrepreneur you'll be faced with many "opportunities" to sacrifice. You'll face the sacrifice of "time" and perhaps, "family relationships". You may even be faced with having to sacrifice your own salary to cover payroll for your employees. But, as a Christian, there should be no question about your willingness to sacrifice for the right reasons.

Paul told the Christians at the church in Rome *"Therefore, I urge you, brothers, in view of God's mercy, to offer your bodies as living sacrifices, holy and pleasing to God—this is your spiritual act of worship."* (Romans 12:1). This passage doesn't just apply to us when we're "in church". This should be an integral part of who we are and how we live.

Commitment

(Defined as: the state of being obligated) I am reminded of when God spoke to Ananias in Acts 9:15-16 when He told him to go to Paul and teach him and baptize him. Ananias was being asked to go to (not run from) someone who had been persecuting the Christians. He did it. Why? Because he was committed to God. God calls us to commitment, not comfort.

As an entrepreneur you will face many challenging situations. You should establish, before you start your business, where your loyalties and commitments lie. You can do what is right, or what is convenient (we have all had plenty of those bosses!). The choice is yours.

Passion/Desire

(Defined as: A strong liking for or devotion to some activity, object or idea; to long or hope for) Many entrepreneurs say the source of their drive to start a business is the "passion" or the desire they have to take control, be their own boss or make lots of money. You might recall that we discussed "motivation" in Chapter 1: Situation Analysis, but the Christian should realize that making their desire for God should be their first priority.

Look at Acts 21: 13-14 when Paul said, *" Paul answered, 'Why are you weeping and breaking my heart? I am ready not only to be bound, but also to die in Jerusalem for the name of the Lord Jesus.' ¹⁴When he would not be dissuaded, we gave up and said, "The Lord's will be done."'*.

I remember when my close friend called to tell me about a job opportunity and I reminded her that "I'm President of my own company. I don't need to find a job!" Calmly, but firmly, she reminded me that my company was failing and I had a family to think of and care for, not to mention the fact that my service as a Christian was suffering. Thank God that He gave me the opportunity to start over and rebuild the relationships that were so important to me - and Him.

Passion must be channeled into the right efforts.

Compassion

(Defined as: Sympathetic consciousness of another's distress together with a desire to alleviate it) H.W. Beecher is reported to have said, "Compassion will cure more sins than condemnation." You will be tempted as an entrepreneur to feel obligated to be "firm" and "boss-like" as you start and grow your business. That is understandable since you are facing an environment which is new to you. And, in truth, there are times when being firm are called for. But not every time! Our reactions may be to deal with any challenging situation like the bosses we have had in the past may have dealt with them.

But, take a lesson from one of the most compassionate leaders the world has ever known - Christ. In John 8:7, Christ was faced with a situation that, per the law, required serious consequences (stoning a woman to death). He reminded the

Pharisees (and the disciples who were looking on) of how to deal with a situation, *"When they kept on questioning him, he straightened up and said to them, 'If any one of you is without sin, let him be the first to throw a stone at her.'"*

As an entrepreneur facing a difficult situation, put yourself into the situation and determine the BEST solution, not necessarily the one that is expected. I am not suggesting you be weak. We know that Christ was not weak at all. But, like Christ, show compassion whenever possible.

Standards

(Defined as: Something established by authority, custom or general consent as a model or example) As a leader your employees expect, and need, guidance. We addressed the importance of establishing clear, well-defined job descriptions, processes and KPI's (Key Performance Indicators) at length in "Chapter 5: Launch" . Establishing and following clear guidelines and expectations is CRITICAL to the success of your business.

Christ had them. He said in Matthew 28:18-20
"18 Then Jesus came to them and said, 'All authority in heaven and on earth has been given to me. 19 Therefore go and make disciples of all nations, baptizing them in[a] the name of the Father and of the Son and of the Holy Spirit, 20 and teaching them to obey everything I have

commanded you. And surely I am with you always, to the very end of the age.'" Christ commanded all men in every nation to <u>go</u>, to <u>make disciples</u>, to <u>baptize</u>, to <u>teach</u> them to 'OBSERVE ALL THINGS I HAVE COMMANDED YOU'. That is a pretty straightforward statement.

There are rules that Christ expects all men to follow. As an entrepreneur, it is your job to make the rules and insure that they are followed. If the rules are not being followed, either the employee is unaware of the rule, choosing to not follow the rule (and needs to be encouraged to get back in line) or the rule needs to be adjusted. Check all options before you make a decision on how to proceed. After all, we are just people, unlike Christ who did not have to adjust the rules - He was perfect!

Servant

(Defined as: To be of use; to stand by; to furnish or supply something needed or desired; to answer the needs of; to provide services that benefit or help) Many entrepreneurs may think of this as applying to their employees, and it does. However, it has been said that "service without reward is punishment".

As an entrepreneur, remember that you have a responsibility to serve others - your family, your customers, your employers and those around you. But, the Messiah gave us, through His message to His disciples, the clearest direction on the subject when

He said, "*²Jesus called them together and said, 'You know that the rulers of the Gentiles lord it over them, and their high officials exercise authority over them. ²⁶Not so with you. Instead, whoever wants to become great among you must be your servant, ²⁷and whoever wants to be first must be your slave— ²⁸just as the Son of Man did not come to be served, but to serve, and to give his life as a ransom for many.'*" (Mathew 20:25-28). This passage seems to challenge the "Be the Boss" mindset. As you take on the role of "boss", remember that the best boss is one who does not expect to be served, but to serve.

Leadership

(Defined as: Position at the front. Vanguard-the forefront of an action or movement.) Someone once said that, "A leader is someone with extraordinary determination." This sums up the typical entrepreneur. Entrepreneurs and small business owners see the goal and are determined to reach that goal.

But there is another side to leadership. The true leader must instill a vision in the minds-eye of those around him to share in that determination; to envision the goal and become committed to reaching it with the "boss". Did you ever feel that way with any of your former "bosses"? Now you have the chance to be that kind of leader. Remember what another wise philosopher said, "Followers will never go any farther than their leader."

I am reminded of the example we used in Stage 5: Launch, in which an entrepreneur/owner is compared to the driver of a stage coach. Your role is to stay above the fray and look forward with vision and guidance, remembering the responsibility to those with whom you work and those riding in the coach - your stakeholders. They have placed their faith and confidence in you to reach the intended destination.

Christ was the ultimate leader. He possessed all the characteristics we have described here - and much, much more. In fact, John reminds us that, *"³⁰Jesus did many other miraculous signs in the presence of his disciples, which are not recorded in this book. ³¹But these are written that you may[a] believe that Jesus is the Christ, the Son of God, and that by believing you may have life in his name."* (John 20:30-31)

Some additional ideas to consider:
- Describe how your spiritual life influences your personal life.
- Explain how you expect it to impact/influence your business.
- Do you attend a religious service on a regular basis?
- Do you hold any special functions (teach, song leader, etc.)?

- How active are you in the activities of your local religious organization?
- Do you believe that having a spiritual foundation is important to your personal success in life?
- How often and how much do you study the Bible?
- How would you describe your faith?
- What is the best thing about having a strong spiritual faith?

As you start this adventure of becoming your own boss, remember three things...

1. **Look UP**-God is there to help you. Develop a relationship with Him so He recognizes your voice when you pray to Him!
2. **Look OUTWARD**: Look out for your neighbor (which includes your employees, customers, suppliers, lenders/investors) - and every other stakeholder.
3. **Look INWARD**: Always examine your motives and your actions before making your decisions.

These three points are summed up in a statement made by Jesus in Matthew 22: 36-40: *"Teacher, which is the greatest commandment in the Law?" 37Jesus replied:" Love the Lord your God with all your heart and with all your soul and with all your mind.' (Look UP!) 38This is the first and greatest commandment. 39And the second is like it: 'Love your neighbor (Look OUTWARD!) as yourself.' (Look INWARD!) All the Law and the Prophets hang on these two commandments."*

And they form the foundation of a successful business venture.

What you have read is simply the sharing of the messages I have learned because of the experiences that God has guided me through. God has already provided the road map. His Word provides the direction and guidance we need to start and grow a successful business.

The Bottom Line...

As an entrepreneur you cannot, should not and do not have to be all by yourself. Surround yourself with professionals who want you to be successful, and especially, have the One who is all-knowing on your team. Give Him the praise and glory for your successes.

Resources

eBay Trends
National Dialogue on Entrepreneurship
Pew Internet and American Life Project
Small Business Administration Office of Advocacy

State Economic Profiles

U.S. Self-Employment

Small Business Economy

Small Business Computing

Small Business Trends Blog

Business Opportunities Weblog
    Source:
http://www.score.org/small_biz_stats.html)

*"The Big Idea: How to Make Your Entrepreneurial Dreams
Come True, From the Aha Moment to Your First Million"*
By: Donny Deutsch (Author), Catherine Whitney
(Author)

"E-Myth Revisited" by Michael Gerber
SBDC
SCORE:

- *See sample Cash Flow Statement in the SCORE-ActivePlans Financial Plan Model (Version 6_08) @*
  - *http://www.score.org/template_gallery.html (Go to: www.Score.org>>Business Tools>>Template Gallery>>Financial Forecast (Provided by ActivePlans))*
- *See sample Income Statements in the SCORE-ActivePlans Financial Plan Model (Version 6_08) @*
  - *http://www.score.org/template_gallery.html (Go to: www.Score.org>>Business Tools>>Template Gallery>>Financial Forecast (Provided by ActivePlans))*
- *See sample Balance Sheets in the SCORE-ActivePlans Financial Plan Model (Version 6_08) @*
  - *http://www.score.org/template_gallery.html (Go to: www.Score.org>>Business Tools>>Template Gallery>>Financial Forecast (Provided by ActivePlans))*
- *See sample Key Ratio Spreadsheet in the SCORE-ActivePlans Financial Plan Model (Version 6_08) @*
  - *http://www.score.org/template_gallery.html (Go to: www.Score.org>>Business Tools>>Template Gallery>>Financial Forecast (Provided by ActivePlans)*
- *Business Plan Pro*
- *Marketing Plan Pro*
- *One Minute Business Plan*

- *Training: How to Write a Business Plan (SBDC), Finance (SBDC); Legal; Others TBD*
- *Resources*
  - *SBDC- (www.northhoustonbusiness.com)*
  - *UH-SBDC- (www.sbdc.uh.edu)*
  - *SCORE- (http://www.score.org/template_gallery.html)*
    - *See sample Cash Flow Statement in the SCORE-ActivePlans Financial Plan Model (Version 6_08) @ http://www.score.org/template_gallery.html (Go to: www.Score.org>>Business Tools>>Template Gallery>>Financial Forecast (Provided by ActivePlans))*
    - *See sample Income Statements in the SCORE-ActivePlans Financial Plan Model (Version 6_08) @ http://www.score.org/template_gallery.html (Go to: www.Score.org>>Business Tools>>Template Gallery>>Financial Forecast (Provided by ActivePlans))*
    - *See sample Balance Sheets in the SCORE-ActivePlans Financial Plan Model (Version 6_08) @ http://www.score.org/template_gallery.html (Go to: www.Score.org>>Business Tools>>Template*

> *Gallery>>Financial Forecast*
> *(Provided by ActivePlans))*
>
> - *See sample Key Ratio Spreadsheet in the SCORE-ActivePlans Financial Plan Model (Version 6_08) @*
>   > *http://www.score.org/template_gall ery.html (Go to: www.Score.org>>Business Tools>>Template Gallery>>Financial Forecast (Provided by ActivePlans))*

- *Articles: www.Aboutr.com - Human Resources*
- *Articles: www.ezinearticles.com*
- *Sample Strategic and Business Plans: www.planware.org*
- *Palo Alto- Business Plan Pro (http://www.paloalto.com/business_plan_softwa re/)*
- *BPlans.com (http://articles.bplans.com/index.php/business- articles/writing-a-business-plan/a-standard- business-plan-outline/)*
- *Investopedia-What is a Cash Flow Statement? http://www.investopedia.com/articles/04/0331 04.asp*
- *Introduction to Cash Flow management (Accounting Coach.com) http://www.accountingcoach.com/online- accounting-course/06Xpg01.html*
- *How to read a cash flow statement: http://www.moneychimp.com/articles/financials /cashflow.htm*

- *Foolish Fundamentals: The Cash Flow Statement: http://www.fool.com/investing/general/2007/09/05/foolish-fundamentals-the-cash-flow-statement.aspx*
- *Great site for free excel spreadsheets- Jaxworks Small Business Spreadsheet Factory: http://www.jaxworks.com/index.htm*
- *Business articles and templates: http://www.bnet.com/*
- *Definitions and examples: Investopedia: (http://www.investopedia.com/terms/r/ratioanalysis.asp)*
- *Crowdfunding: http://en.wikipedia.org/wiki/Crowd_funding*

www.ingramcontent.com/pod-product-compliance
Lightning Source LLC
Chambersburg PA
CBHW030934220326
41521CB00040B/2318